Moving the Classroom Outdoors

Moving the Classroom Outdoors

Schoolyard-Enhanced Learning in Action

Herbert W. Broda

Stenhouse
PUBLISHERS

www.stenhouse.com

Stenhouse Publishers
www.stenhouse.com

Credits:
Page 5: Figure 1.1 designed by Jeremy Solin. Used with permission.
Pages 92–95: Material adapted from *Twenty/Twenty: Projects and Activities for Wild School Sites* by Paul Schiff, Ohio Department of Natural Resources, Wild School Site Project. Copyright © 1996. Reprinted with permission.
Pages 117-118: Material adapted from the Web site of the Boston Schoolyard Initiative (BSI). Used with permission.

Photo Credits:
Donnan Stoicovy: Figure 2.60 and portrait photo in Spotlight 3, "Professional Development, Park Forest Style"
Liz Penner: Figures 3.9 a, b, c and 3.10
Sarah Palmer: Figures 2.38 and 2.39
Granny's Garden School: Photographs in Spotlight 5, "Granny's Garden School"
Mary Beth Cary: Figure 2.19

Cover photo by Travis Hall
All other photos are by Herb Broda and Matthew Broda

Library of Congress Cataloging-in-Publication Data

Broda, Herbert W., 1945–
  Moving the classroom outdoors : schoolyard-enhanced learning in action
/ Herbert W. Broda.
    p. cm.
  ISBN 978-1-57110-791-6 (pbk.) — ISBN 978-1-57110-915-6 (e-book)
 1. Outdoor learning laboratories. 2. Outdoor education. I. Title.
  LB1047.B758 2011
  372.13'84—dc22

                                        2011007000

Cover, interior design, and typeset by Designboy Creative Group

Manufactured in the United States of America

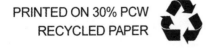

PRINTED ON 30% PCW
RECYCLED PAPER

17 16 15   9 8 7 6 5 4 3 2

If a child is to keep alive his inborn sense of wonder...
he needs the companionship of at least one adult who can share it,
rediscovering with him the joy, excitement and mystery of the world we live in.

—Rachel Carson

To educators around the globe who are passionate
about helping children to nurture their inborn sense of wonder:
You are an awesome blessing to the planet!

Contents

Foreword

The more we put concrete, drywall, and steel between us and the natural world, the more we lose important elements of our humanity, and our humanity is the key to successful teaching and learning. Let's heed Herb Broda's call and shrink the distance. Practical though his earlier *Schoolyard-Enhanced Learning* was, *Moving the Classroom Outdoors* blows away all lingering excuses and makes the dream achievable.

Inviting at every turn, Herb provides an amazing array of pros, cons, research, and keen insight on how to make the outdoors a compelling teaching ally, not just an add-on to an already overburdened curriculum and teaching load. The evidence of learning outcomes that he demonstrates in the book are the very same twenty-first-century skills and content that experts claim are vital to students' success.

Every page is steeped in reality and bursting with innovation. Herb dives deeply, providing specific details, vivid examples, and critical thinking about integrating the indoors with the outdoors in rural, suburban, and urban classrooms, even in locations where there is no space to do it. As Herb shows us, our goal is for students to interact with the outdoors, not just beautify it, and to use it as both the vehicle for integrating curriculum and as content

itself, ultimately inspiring powerful stewardship in the next generation.

Wisely, Herb begins by showing us how to prepare ourselves and the outdoors for student interaction and curriculum. This includes robust justification for those who hesitate to embrace the dynamic instruction teaching outdoors provides. He continues with specific "tips and tricks, gimmicks and grabbers" from the seasoned pro that he is and from the many classroom teachers he's worked with or interviewed.

The first call of many educators when taking on a new endeavor or mind-set is, "Show me what it looks like," and here the call is answered fully. Herb describes outdoor site inventories, communication options, tips on how to involve those inside and outside the building, the impact of foot-traffic patterns, time factors, suggestions for long-term commitment to outdoor sites, class management tips, safety concerns, advice on working with volunteers, and fund-raising ideas—all of these and much more are included in these pages. Finally, Herb includes case studies of schools that have successful outdoor learning programs and includes their contact information so we can follow up with them.

Moving the Classroom Outdoors provides more useful information to teachers and principals than many other books in this genre combined. Particularly impressive is Herb's special focus chapters on urban classrooms and incorporating technology, the latter of which benefits from the insightful work of Matthew Broda, Herb's son. Matthew also served as primary photographer for many of the classrooms and schools represented, and his photos create the sense that all this is doable.

No pun intended, but wow, Herb's done the fieldwork so we don't have to, and we are grateful. He dismantles every roadblock and provides clever dynamics for motivating staff, parents, and students to connect with the outdoors and improve learning. He reveals a wonderful, pedagogical palette that surrounds all of us, if we'd only open our eyes. In a world in which students are drowning in screens of all sizes, *Moving the Classroom Outdoors* is the collective canoe, paddle, and compass heading for the positive venture ahead. What a gift!

Were Rachel Carson to meet Herb Broda today, I'm sure she'd smile, shake his hand, and declare, "Well done, Herb." It's up to the rest of us to make good on all that Rachel Carson inspires, and all that Herb Broda makes possible.

—Rick Wormeli

Acknowledgments

It's difficult to know where to begin. *Moving the Classroom Outdoors: School-yard-Enhanced Learning in Action* is based on conversations—many conversations. Dozens of interviews as well as casual discussions with hundreds of teachers, administrators, students, parents, agency staff, and project developers at thirty schools, nature centers, and schoolyard "greening" organizations in the United States and Canada provided the practical focus and tangible examples of outdoor learning in action. Although it's not practical, or even possible, to list everyone who contributed to this project, I feel that several folks should be recognized by name.

My first daunting challenge was the selection of schools and organizations for site visits. The following people were of tremendous assistance in helping me locate exemplary school sites and programs:

Kristin Metz, Boston Schoolyard Initiative

Kim Bailey, Environmental Education in Georgia

Jen Dennison, Ohio Department of Natural Resources, Division of Wildlife

Grant Parkins, North Carolina Botanical Garden, Chapel Hill, North Carolina

Cheryl Bauer-Armstrong, Earth Partnership for Schools, Madison, Wisconsin

Jeremy Solin, LEAF Forestry Education Program, Stevens Point, The Wisconsin K–12 Forestry Education Program

Tim Grant, coeditor of *Green Teacher*, Toronto, Canada

Kirk Meyer, Green Schoolyard Network, Wayland, Massachusetts
Cam Collyer and Samara Newman, Evergreen, Toronto, Canada

As I toured schools I met several people who had inspiring stories that needed to be told. These are people who personify outdoor education and have focused their careers on helping children connect with nature. Although many others could have been included, the realities of page limitations resulted in six individuals being featured in the Spotlights sections of this book. Meeting these folks and hearing their stories was both moving and humbling. My own perspective of outdoor learning was refined and energized by these educators who exemplify a love of nature and passion about outdoor teaching and learning:

Georgia Gómez-Ibáñez, retired teacher/active volunteer, Cambridge, Wisconsin

Toni Hill, former principal of Forest View Elementary, Durham, North Carolina

Fritz Monroe, principal of Brookside Elementary, Worthington, Ohio

Donnan Stoicovy, principal of Park Forest Elementary, State College, Pennsylvania

Roberta Paolo, founder of Granny's Garden School, Loveland, Ohio

Catherine Padgett, teacher, Ford Elementary, Acworth, Georgia

I want to acknowledge several other educators who gave significant time to provide site tours, plan school visits, arrange faculty interviews, and/or submit photos and resource materials: Eleanor Ashton, Marianne Ayoob, Jamie Barnhill, Diane Beckett, Rebecca Burns, Heidi Campbell, Mary Beth Cary, Neil Clay, Ann Coffey, Terry Deal, Nancy Flexner, Marylu Flowers-Schoen, Susan Gottfried, John Heffernan, Myrna Johnson, Betty Jue, Sally Massengale, Florence Milutinovic, Bob Palmatier, Sarah Palmer, Liz Penner, Peggy Pepper, Ayschia Saiymeh, Kimberly Schafer, Bob Schlaefer, Mary Sheridan, Carol Sowers, Kathy Stapleton, Sarah Tichnor, Matt Tiller, and Karan Wood.

I know that there are names that I have missed, and I apologize for that. In addition to the persons named above, dozens of other folks took the time to talk about their programs and provided additional richness and reality to the content of this book. Please realize that everyone's input, even in the form of a quick chat in the hall or a conversation over dinner, has become part of the fabric of this book.

My semester-long senior faculty study leave provided by Ashland University was greatly appreciated and pivotal. This significant block of open time made it possible for me to visit schools in the United States and Canada during the school year while faculty and students were present.

Once again, Bill Varner, senior editor at Stenhouse, has worked his magic! Bill's creativity, encouragement, and practical insights are reflected throughout the book. The amazing editorial talents and practical suggestions of Erin Trainer, Stenhouse freelance copyeditor, are reflected on every page, skillfully polishing the manuscript into its final form. Thanks also to Jay Kilburn, production manager at Stenhouse. Jay's enthusiasm for the book and his vision and creativity for the graphic design elements have made this a pleasant book to hold.

I want to say a special thank-you to my son Matthew, who served as a photographer during several school visits and who wrote the technology chapter. Father-son professional collaboration involves different dynamics than working with a colleague down the hall. I am so thankful that we had this unique and enriching opportunity.

Finally, I am so blessed to have a loving family that supports and truly enjoys one another. My wife, Janet, is undoubtedly the most patient and understanding person I have ever known. Her constant support for my projects and dreams has been energizing and sustaining. Our three children, Emily, Matthew, and Michael, are also amazing people. They were delightfully enthusiastic children who have grown to be encouraging, loving, and thoughtful adults. Sharing nature with this wonderful family has always been my idea of a perfect day.

Introduction

Since the publication in 2007 of *Schoolyard-Enhanced Learning: Using the Outdoors as an Instructional Tool, K–8*, there has been a steady increase in all things green. Although I wish I could take the credit, the reality is that political, social, and economic forces have become aligned in a curious way to create a unique turn-of-the-century environmental movement. Headlines, podcasts, blogs, and TV specials regularly deliver topics related to energy efficiency, environmental impact, alternative energy sources, and even nature awareness.

Many schools have also picked up on the new environmental movement. Teachers who previously struggled to advocate for more outdoor learning experiences are now finding themselves in the mainstream. Green is good at school also. No more need to convince people that going outside is good for kids—schoolyard learning programs are now proudly featured as unique elements of a school's curriculum. Of course, schools always stress that outdoor learning must be carefully linked to academic content, but that's OK. Research studies continue to show that a mix of outdoor instruction and indoor teaching leads to improved achievement (Place-Based Education Evaluation Collaborative 2011; Children and Nature Network 2011; Lieberman and Hoody 1998).

This book is designed to help schools explore how to make the school grounds more useful for instruction. I want to be clear that I have not tried to create a major, all-inclusive tome that is the final word on schoolyard enhancement. Many books already exist that go into enormous detail regarding species selection and planting techniques, sophisticated site mapping methods, and exotic landscape design elements. Although detailed technical guides may be very helpful to schools that are already well under way with schoolyard enhancement planning, too much detail, especially about enhancements that are simply not economically or locally feasible, can discourage schools that still have a lot of questions and are not ready to plunge into complex schoolwide projects.

Rather than try to be everything to people at all levels of interest in outdoor instruction, I have tried to design this book for the explorer—the teacher or principal who is intrigued by the benefits of outdoor learning and wants to give it a try or wants to expand some initial projects. The focus is on basic elements and features that can be accomplished rather inexpensively, do not depend on extensive help from outside consultants, and do not necessarily require that an entire faculty be solidly committed to outdoor learning.

This is a book filled with examples—examples of exemplary schools and inspiring people. More than seventy people met with me at approximately thirty schools, nature centers, and schoolyard "greening" organizations in eight states and Canada. Photos have been carefully selected to provide a visual interpretation of the good ideas that were found everywhere. This book is intended to be a companion volume to *Schoolyard-Enhanced Learning* (Broda 2007). While *Schoolyard-Enhanced Learning* provides a general introduction to the benefits, research, background, rationale, and basic tips for outdoor learning, *Moving the Classroom Outdoors* focuses strongly on a plethora of examples that show schoolyard-enhanced learning in action.

Chapter 1
Preparing to Use the Outdoors

Elementary principal Fritz Monroe calls it "dreamstorming." What a great term to describe a process that inspires people to think creatively about outdoor learning options! Whether it's a full committee or just a teacher or two, people work best when they are challenged to dream and create rather than simply approve a preconceived project.

This chapter focuses on several critical items that need to be considered early in the dreamstorming phase, even before any nails are pounded or seeds planted. Although overplanning can drag down a project and drain enthusiasm, most problems occur because there has not been enough preliminary thought given to a variety of important elements. Whether you are a teacher who will be the one and only on your staff to try outdoor learning or you are the catalyst who is enthusiastically bringing together an entire staff to use the school grounds, there are common issues, concerns, and cautions that need to be considered.

Starting the Process

Outdoor learning projects begin in a variety of ways. Some seem to spring almost spontaneously into existence with a schoolwide groundswell of excitement.

Others are quietly proposed by one or two interested folks, who then gently nurture the concept and inspire others to try outdoor teaching simply by modeling effective practice.

The initial impetus sometimes comes from administrators. Twenty years ago, one Ohio elementary school principal was inspired by an unused retention pond on his school grounds. He saw the potential for outdoor learning and has been encouraging the use of the outdoors for more than two decades. The retention pond is now a frequently used learning laboratory and is only one feature of more than a dozen that have been added to the site over the years. Even his office has a nature theme, including a resident snake (although on the day I visited, the small ball python had escaped!).

Parents also can serve as the initiating force for outdoor learning. One Georgia elementary school greening project was initiated by a small group of parents who wanted to help teachers have the resources that they needed to teach on the school grounds. A subcommittee of the parent/teacher organization surveyed teachers to find out their interests in outdoor learning. Attempts were also made to learn what materials and additions to the site would be needed in order to bring teachers and students outdoors. The parent group took the survey results and diligently began to tackle the needs and concerns that were mentioned. The result was the creation of ten outdoor classroom teaching areas and numerous site enhancements on the grounds.

Although administrators and parents can serve as initiators of outdoor learning projects, most outdoor enhancements are inspired by teachers. Often a teacher has attended a professional development event which introduced the concept of learning in the outdoors. In North Carolina, teachers from three different buildings attended a summer outdoor learning institute. As a result, these teachers returned to their schools energized and continually sustained by the network that they established with one another at the conference.

Site Inventory

Some type of site inventory is usually the starting point for any schoolyard enhancement project—large or small. Of course, if the project is only to plant a small container garden and place it outside your classroom door, the site inventory can be completed in a matter of minutes. However, if the project involves several classrooms, landscape-altering enhancements, or significant space on the school grounds, it's well worth the time to do an in-depth site inventory.

The basic purpose of a site inventory, whether for a small or large project, is to answer these questions:

1. What already exists in the area to be enhanced?
2. Will the project need to be modified to accommodate current or future use of the site?

A map of the site is the best way to begin. (See Figure 1.1 for a sample map.) As you map site features, ideas come to mind and priorities begin to emerge. Here are some general tips for doing a rather comprehensive site inventory for a project that might involve adding outdoor seating areas, pathways, and gardens to the school site. A map could include the following:

- Existing buildings, driveways, parking areas, sidewalks, play equipment, playing fields for sports, swales (low, moist areas, often with profuse plant growth), and retention ponds
- Areas of heavy foot traffic that are not paved

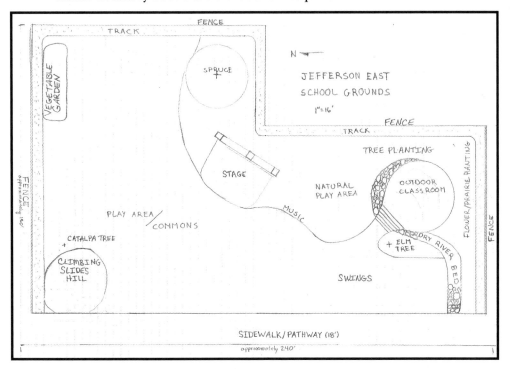

Figure 1.1 This simple, hand-drawn site map provides a clear image of how proposed features could be incorporated into the existing site.

- Access to water faucets and electricity
- Areas with erosion or perennial drainage issues
- Existing underground utility lines
- Trees
- Existing landscaped areas or unused garden beds
- Areas where vandalism has been, or could be, a problem
- Playground areas
- Any unusual topographic features, such as large boulders or ditches

The site map doesn't have to be beautiful; it just needs to show the location of existing and planned elements in relation to one another. You don't want to set up a teaching/meeting area near an area of heavy foot traffic or a noisy playground.

In addition to the preceding items, it is very useful to inventory the natural features of the site. It's worth your time to do the following:

Contact a naturalist from a local nature center or park to walk the site with you and identify the existing plant species on the grounds. It's often amazing how many varieties of plants and animals you may already have on your site. A naturalist can help you determine what native, nonnative, and invasive species exist on your grounds.

Check with a garden club or master gardener if you are planning to construct garden plots. You need to determine soil type, drainage, and any other special needs that will have to be met before you plant anything.

Do a shade analysis. Depending on your plans, the need for shade or sun can determine where certain enhancements are placed. Give thought to where the sun will be during the majority of the school day, especially when planning a teaching/meeting area.

History and Existing Plans for the Building and Site

Check about future expansion plans for the building and the school site. Even small construction projects can cause problems. At one Ohio school, children worked diligently during the spring to plant a butterfly garden only to find it destroyed in August because a retention wall had been replaced over the summer.

Research the history of the site. What was here before the school was built? A local historical society can often provide an abundance of interesting local lore. One school discovered that it was on a site used as an encampment during the Civil War. Also, research the types of plants and animals that would have lived on the site prior to development. Understanding the natural and social history of the area can inspire the development of unique activities that can help children develop a unique sense of place. Whenever possible, have students help with research into the natural and cultural history of the site.

Keeping Everyone in the Loop

Catherine Padgett of Ford Elementary in Georgia puts it very well: "Every year you have to resell outdoor learning." How true. Every year there are new families entering the school, new faculty members, and experienced faculty who may need to be encouraged again to use the outdoors. People need to be regularly reminded of the power of outdoor learning.

Communication is critical, regardless of who starts the outdoor learning initiative. Whether the project is only a few birdfeeders outside your classroom window or a large amphitheater on a convenient slope, it is essential that the administration be a part of the planning.

Even for a small project, it's essential to focus upon these items:
- A rationale for doing the project or site enhancement
- A time line or schedule for accomplishing the project
- A clear connection with the curriculum

It's important to provide these items in written form. Because administrators are bombarded with dozens of "great ideas" each week, principals appreciate a document that contains the salient points for future reference.

Communication is also equally important if the administrator is the initiator of the project. Top-down projects are always risky and certainly require intentional inclusion of all staff in the planning process. In addition, thoroughly explain how teachers' efforts will be supported and what resources will be available. When an administrator initiates an outdoor learning project, it is essential that a teacher committee be established to provide the nuts and bolts suggestions and cautions that will make or break a project.

The beauty of outdoor teaching is that it does not require that an entire grade level or faculty be sold on the idea. As long as you have administra-

tive approval, you can do a lot of outdoor learning activities on your own. If, however, you want to make enhancements such as gardens, pathways, and outdoor learning stations to the school site, it is tremendously helpful to have wide involvement in the process.

Committees

Committees can serve a valuable communications function for an outdoor learning initiative. For small projects, such as establishing an herb garden or creating an outdoor teaching/meeting area, a small committee of interested teachers, and anyone directly affected by the changes (e.g., custodial staff, administrators, etc.), is sufficient. Larger projects, of course, require representation from all of the potential stakeholders as well as potential sources of help.

Planning for large projects seems to work best when the project initiators and the building administrator meet initially to set broad goals for the project and then select who should be invited to join the committee. Committees for large, schoolwide projects involving significant site enhancements could include representation from the following:

- Building administration
- District and building maintenance staff
- Appropriate specialists (e.g., naturalists to help develop trails, persons knowledgeable in local safety codes if structures such as gazebos or sun shelters are being constructed)
- Parent groups
- Teachers of all grade levels or content areas
- Students

Be generous with your invitations to join the planning committee. Jen Dennison of the Ohio Department of Natural Resources recommends extending invitations to clerical, custodial, and cafeteria staff. A group representing many aspects of the school's operation creates a richness of thinking that can spawn ideas that would never have occurred to just teachers and administrators.

Neighbors living near the school can be a great addition to a planning committee, or they should at least be made aware of the plans. Jen tells the story of a school that had placed compost piles at the back of the school grounds. Soon it became obvious that trash was being tossed on the pile as well. Once neighbors were aware of the composting project, the trash dumping stopped.

Whether the committee is small or large, there should be two critical outcomes from the early meetings. The first is a long-range plan and list of goals for the school site. Two or three long-term goals are fine as long as everyone understands that the goals are subject to addition and revision over time. The second critical outcome is the identification of one or two small projects as a beginning. Even large committees can get into problems when a dozen site enhancements are launched almost simultaneously. It's critical to prioritize and to complete the first enhancements very, very well.

Rather than use one large committee that meets frequently to make dozens of decisions, break up the initial big committee into smaller groups that can work on specific topics, such as fund-raising, construction issues, plant selection, curriculum alignment, and so on. Most people are willing to work on a committee that is charged with a well-defined task but may balk at serving on a general-purpose committee that frequently discusses topics that are of little interest to the individual.

Getting Your Colleagues Involved

Cam Collyer, director of Learning Grounds for Evergreen, is charged with encouraging schools to consider using the school grounds for instruction. He suggests that one of the best ways to inspire others to consider outdoor learning is to literally show what can be done. According to Cam, "Visual presentations are critical. People need to see examples."

It's powerful to show people pictures of what you have in mind. Contact your state or provincial outdoor/environmental education agency and ask for examples of schools that are doing the types of things that you have in mind. Often a school will gladly send you digital photos that you can include in a presentation. Chapter 2 of this book includes many photos of site enhancements from around the United States.

A group visit to a school that has the types of enhancements you are planning is ideal. Actually, a site visit is probably the most effective way to build excitement for a project. Often the ride back from the visit results in animated dialogue that can crystallize a focal point for developing an entire project.

Cam's thoughts are echoed by Jen Dennison of the Ohio Department of Natural Resources. She recommends using outdoor educators from agencies such as departments of natural resources, extension service offices, and soil and water conservation offices to help sell the idea to other faculty members.

Although a short presentation about the benefits of outdoor learning may be a good start, Jen feels that the most powerful way to convince others on a faculty is to do a workshop on their own school grounds. Seeing the possibilities presented on your own site is a powerful motivator. Admittedly, limited professional development meeting time and contractual constraints can make it difficult to hold a two-hour workshop. It's worth pursuing, however, since teachers who have actually tried outdoor activities related to their content areas are often very willing to try more on their own.

Try a half-day workshop on a Saturday. Although you may only have 20 percent of your staff attend, you can be certain that those folks will leave very convinced that outdoor learning is effective. Teacher workshops seem to generate the greatest enthusiasm for outdoor learning.

Although it's important to show examples of site enhancements, it is equally important to show how these additions to the school grounds can help to teach required concepts in the curriculum. It is critical to help colleagues make the leap from thinking of the outdoors as purely enrichment or "extra" experience to seeing outdoor learning experiences as yet another instructional approach to introduce, teach, and/or reinforce concepts in the curriculum.

An interest in outdoor teaching can be cultivated by simply publicizing what other teachers are doing. One North Carolina school uses the traditional morning video news announcement time to incorporate a Science Friday special each week. Students just share some interesting things that they found or saw outside during the week. The same idea would also work well as a simple audio announcement. Nothing sells outdoor learning quicker than excited kids sharing what they are discovering on the school grounds.

Overcoming Stumbling Blocks to Involvement

To those passionate about outdoor teaching, it just doesn't seem possible that anyone would be reluctant to use nature as a backdrop for instruction. For many educators, though, the concept may be interesting, but the questions remain.

Regardless of geographic location, school size, or socioeconomic level of the community, there are always doubts and concerns that are consistently mentioned as barriers to trying outdoor learning. Let's take a look at some of the most commonly mentioned stumbling blocks that I heard from educators in various regions of the United States and Canada.

Time

By far the most frequently mentioned barrier is time—and for very good reason. Follow any dedicated teacher for a day and you quickly feel the pressure and exhaustion that comes from trying to fit complex learning and testing requirements into a tight daily schedule that can change unexpectedly. Understandably, most teachers would be leery of adding anything to the day that could possibly magnify the time squeeze.

North Carolina teacher Sarah Palmer has an answer: "We need to convince people that it's not a matter of more time, just time used differently." For example, if the topic is measurement, terms and units can be explained indoors, followed by an extension experience outdoors to practice the concept by measuring objects on the school grounds. Instead of doing the practice inside, we have just moved it outdoors. Although it may add a few minutes to move kids from indoors to out, the heightened learning and real-world connections certainly compensate.

"But is it *worth* the time?" is an important pedagogical question. A growing number of research studies are clarifying that a combination of indoor and outdoor instruction does result in improved achievement. Both teachers and students find an increased motivation that comes from a change of pace and place.

Two great sources for research showing the impact of outdoor learning on student achievement are the Web sites of the Children and Nature Network (2011) and the Placed-Based Education Evaluation Collaborative (2011).

For some teachers the concern is not only instructional time, but also finding the time outside of the school day to maintain outdoor learning areas. That's a valid concern and needs to be met first by starting with small site enhancements that take little maintenance (e.g., creating a simple teaching/meeting area or setting up a few bird feeders). If more complex projects, like large garden plots or bird blinds, are considered, there simply has to be volunteer help. That topic is addressed later in this chapter.

Curriculum Integration

Interestingly, this stumbling block also is related to time. If the outdoors is not really related to the curriculum, it becomes an extra and therefore soaks up valuable time. I strongly support the philosophy that schoolyard-enhanced

learning should not be used by a teacher unless it is directly related to curricular objectives being taught. It is encouraging, however, to look at the number of grade-level objectives in most content areas that could incorporate meaningful outdoor experiences into their instruction.

All content areas are concerned about developing process skills like observation, classification, inference, comprehension, description, evaluation, comparison, and data analysis. Outdoor activities can provide both the venue and content for practicing these skills.

The concept of using the outdoors as both venue and content is central to visualizing how outdoor learning can be meaningfully incorporated into teaching. The schoolyard can provide a venue, or backdrop, for an activity (e.g., going outside to read a story) or it can provide the content and serve as the essential element of an activity (going outside to find examples of geometric shapes in nature). Either use is valid and complements the curriculum. Sometimes just moving the class outside (venue) to do an activity that could be done indoors provides a needed energy boost. For an objective related to probability and sampling, going outside to sample the number of dandelions on the school grounds (content) can provide an activity just as effective as one done at an indoor desk.

Classroom Management

Many teachers fear that their students will immediately associate the outdoors with play and have difficulty focusing on instructional tasks. Most outdoor educators have had that bad dream of kids running wildly all over the school grounds with the teacher standing helplessly in the distance, clipboard in hand! (Indoor educators experience a similar classroom dream around the middle of August, right before the school year begins.) The key is to make clear your behavior expectations indoors before going outside. Then, as soon as the group is outside in the teaching/meeting area, it's critical to go over the rules again. Here are some other tips that can make working with kids outdoors a little easier:

> *Establish clear boundaries.* Unless you clearly specify physical boundaries, students will tend to move farther and farther away during an activity. Delineate very specifically where the activity should take place: "Don't go beyond the sidewalk" or "Stay in the area enclosed by the trees that I have marked with strips of duct tape."

Use the smallest useful area. When doing most observation or description activities it's really not necessary to have students spread out over a big area. Look at the site and determine what would be the smallest area to use that would still result in an effective activity. The more widely scattered the class, the more time is spent gathering the flock at the end of the activity.

Use a signal to get students' attention. A whistle, bell, or bird call can be an effective signal that tells students to stop what they are doing and listen to you or return to the teaching meeting area.

Meet in a circle. When working with groups in the outdoors, I have found the circle to be the most effective way to communicate. Having kids just stand in a clump invites problems. With the group in a circle, you can see everyone and minimize disruption.

Bring along a backpack or tote. Pack the supplies, books, and materials needed for the activity in a backpack or tote (Figure 1.2) rather than an awkward box. Triple check to make sure that you have everything you need.

Plan a time frame or routine. For example, five minutes to form a circle and hear directions; twenty minutes to do the activity; ten minutes to reflect and share. Although the time frame may vary as a result of unexpected discoveries, having a time frame outlined in advance can dispel some of the uncertainty that teachers new to outdoor teaching often feel.

Figure 1.2 This sturdy canvas tote holds everything needed to begin a study of worms: reference books, teaching aids, handy storage bags, simple digging tools, and disposable gloves. Notice how activities are labeled on the sides of the totes so that they can be easily organized on a shelf.

I have never seen a teacher who has good indoor classroom management have difficulty outdoors. I have also noticed the converse: a teacher who struggles with management issues indoors will most likely run into problems on the school grounds.

As all teachers can verify, however, classes seem to have personalities. An outdoor activity that worked well with last year's class may need to be modified

drastically or even substituted for something else because of this year's personality mix. The same reality exists inside the classroom. We modify and exchange indoor activities based on the type of class that we have at any given time. It's critical to remember that schoolyard-enhanced learning is a teaching technique, not an end in itself. We use the outdoors when it fits best.

Lack of Outdoor Expertise

"I just don't know much about the outdoors" is the reason some teachers are reluctant to step outside. Unless you are using the outdoors to teach biology or other specific science topics, that really shouldn't be a problem. The emphasis of most nonscience outdoor learning activities is to heighten observation skills and to focus on description or other process skills. When there are questions about the names of specific plants or animals, you can always use field guides to answer them. Although there are elementary school children who are very interested in knowing the names of items in nature, I have found that most children are more interested in using their senses to explore what they see.

Some elementary schools have had classes develop field guides that are specific to their own school grounds or community. This type of highly localized field guide can be a huge help to the teacher who wants to be able to answer the "What is it?" questions that do occasionally pop up. Cooperative extension offices, departments of natural resources, and local nature centers often have materials, and sometimes personnel, to help with the development of a local guide.

The Evergreen Community Charter School in Asheville, North Carolina, has made excellent use of student-produced field guide projects. The fourth grade produced a guide titled "Animals of Western North Carolina." Students researched facts about local wildlife, wrote the text, and even included games, drawings, and riddles to better describe the critters they had chosen. The result was a student-produced magazine that was made available in the community. The booklet not only serves as a field guide but also helped to make the community more aware of the school and its mission.

The Evergreen second- and third-grade students produced a different style of local field guide. After making many trips to a local botanical garden, students researched plants and recorded information about the leaves, blossoms, berries, habitat, and so on. Children then drew amazingly descriptive pictures of the plants they had studied. Their observations, measurements, and research about the plants were combined with the drawings to produce a delightful guide that reflects the depth of learning that students gained from this project (Figure 1.3a–d). Although this activity was done at a local park, it would be very possible to make a field guide of plants and animals found on your school site.

Making schoolyard field guides has so much educational value. In addition to focusing on careful observation and description of the natural world, students learn research techniques, develop writing and drawing skills, and become very well acquainted with the flora and fauna that live right outside the door of the classroom.

Safety

Providing children with safe outdoor experiences has to be our highest priority. Every ef-

Figure 1.3a–d Students from the Evergreen Community Charter School in Asheville, North Carolina, incorporated language arts, science, art, and even technology and social studies as they produced these two field guides about plants and animals in their community.

fort has to be made to evaluate outdoor areas to avoid potentially dangerous situations and to make the schoolyard as safe as possible. The most essential ingredient for a safe outdoor experience is a class that understands and follows your rules and expectations for working in the outdoors. Although student accidents while engaged in outdoor learning activities are really quite rare, most occur because a student has not followed an instruction.

Since every site and locale is unique, it's not practical to develop an all-inclusive safety checklist. Teachers generally have an intuitive sense for knowing what might be too risky for any given group. A few general safety

Box Turtles don't have any teeth; instead they have long necks and sharp beaks for eating. A box turtle is the only reptile that has a shell. Box turtles are colored brownish-greenish to camouflage themselves under leaves. The turtle shell is hard and the top part of the shell is called carapace. The underneath is called plastron.

Box turtles are found in the eastern parts of the United States. Box turtles live in shallow streams, mud, and the forest floor. Box turtles can also live under rocks for their homes protection and hibernation.

Box turtle's eat many kinds of plants and insects such as berries, mushrooms, earthworms, slugs, and snails. Box turtles move slowly, so their food must be easy for them to catch. Box turtles use their claws to walk in mud and to catch their food.

Their body temperature depends on the outside weather (what we would call "cold-blooded"). Turtles can control their body temperatures. They can also live longer than most other animals- as much as a hundred years.

The box turtles habitat is being destroyed daily as forests become decimated. If we keep cutting down all the trees the box turtles won't have a place for feeding, hibernating, mating, and living. Although the box turtle is not at this time an endangered species, global warming, habitat destruction, and erosion will eventually affect this reptile. Already pollution is impacting my animal because my animal drinks from the polluted water. We can help keep this reptile safe by replanting trees and through better forest management.

By: Dallas Moffat

I have a shell that doesn't come off
I am a reptile
I eat many kinds of plants and insects
Who am I?

Figure 1.3b

categories, though, should be mentioned:

Awareness of individual student health or mobility issues that may be affected by outdoor involvement. For example, allergies, breathing difficulties, or physical impairments of students need to be considered when planning activities.

General condition of the outdoor area. Scan the area for broken glass or other dangerous material and know the location of noxious plants like poison ivy and the location of hives and nests of unpleasant insects. Also be aware of any spraying or other chemical usage in the area where you will be.

Procedures for using equipment. If students will be using tools or equipment for planting or other site enhancement efforts, it's essential to demonstrate proper use of the tools and be sure that they are age-appropriate.

General precautions. Take along a cell phone or a radio. Have another adult along if you will be a distance from the school building. Try to keep all students in your view during an activity.

Check Before You Dig

Before going too far in the planning of larger site enhancement projects like gazebos, hillside amphitheaters, water features, or even bird blinds, be sure to

Tree: White Oak

     Deciduous, 80-100 ft.

Leaves: Simple structure, untoothed edges, lobed shaped leaves.
Green color above and gray below, smooth texture.
Alternate position. 7 inches long by 2 inches wide.

Bark: light gray, rough texture.

Acorns: Light gray on bottom and dark brown on the top, 3/8 in.
1 1\4 in. Appear in winter.

Habitat: Sunny and shady wooded areas.

Plant: Wild Geranium

     15 in. tall.

Leaves: Palmate structure, toothed edges, lobed shaped leaves.
Green/gray, and fuzzy. 4 in. long.

Stem: 15 in. long.

Flowers: Bloom April – June.

     1 in., pink, simple flowers. 5 petals per flower. Has
fragrance.

Seeds: Elongated shape.

Habitat: Sunny or shady, wooded or open areas.

Figure 1.3c & 1.3d

check with building *and* district-level administration. Often there are zoning, construction code, or liability insurance requirements that need to be considered when alterations are made to a school site. It's best to check early in the process rather than have an excited planning committee learn that weeks of effort were in vain. Even garden plots located beside buildings need to be approved by the district maintenance staff. There is a possibility that gardens located too near a building can cause drainage problems.

It's always good practice to contact utilities or communication networks like Dig Safe to confirm that underground water and power lines are not in the area. The few minutes it takes to verify that it's OK to dig can prevent a project from being scuttled on the very first day.

Parent/Volunteer Involvement

One Ohio parent pointed out that schoolyard volunteering provides unique options for the "not so typical" parent volunteer. Although she is perfectly happy to spend a few hours weeding flower beds, she is not interested at all in attending traditional parent/teacher association meetings. In today's increasingly busy and scheduled society, there probably are many like-minded parents who would love to help out if there were tasks that could be done as personal time permits. There are certainly many parents who are eager to be involved beyond just providing cupcakes for a class party or attending monthly evening meetings. In an attempt to generate more parent assistance, schools may need to try some innovative incentives that benefit families as well as the school site. For example, parents could receive reduced tuition for the school's after-school program if they help to maintain the outdoor classroom. Families can even work together to trim, weed, and do minor maintenance in the schoolyard.

To be very blunt, it is simply impossible to implement and sustain a multifaceted and multiclassroom outdoor learning program without the help of parents and other community volunteers.

Getting Parents Involved

Most parents really enjoy taking part in the programs and activities of their children's school. Outdoor learning is an especially appealing avenue for including parents because it provides a very different set of opportunities for involvement than are needed indoors. After parents understand the "what" and "why" of outdoor learning, they frequently can see a variety of ways to contribute.

Show Connections
First, parents need to understand why you are emphasizing outdoor instruction. It's critical to help parents see the educational benefits of outdoor learning and to clearly show how outdoor instruction relates to the school's curriculum. Some schools have parents take part in a sample outdoor activity as part of a parent group meeting. As the activity is debriefed, parents quickly see the value of outdoor learning and its connection to academic content.

Survey Parents

Put together a quick survey to find out interests, hobbies, or special training that parents may have to contribute to the development of learning enhancements on the school site. Be sure to query about technical and construction skills as well as nature-related interests. One survey included a question asking parents for names of clubs or organizations that they thought might be interested in donating some volunteer time or resources.

Use Visuals to Promote

Use parent/teacher conference days, grandparent days, or any other times when parents and community folks visit the building as opportunities to showcase how your students are engaged in outdoor learning. A simple slide show can be strategically placed near a meeting area or in a busy hallway or reception area. The simplicity of taking and editing video clips makes it very doable to create a brief video to show at a variety of events or to run continuously in an entry or reception area. One school conducts parent conferences in classrooms and runs a video in the hall as parents wait to talk with the teacher.

Recently, I visited a school that was using student-produced podcasts to highlight outdoor learning activities at the school. The podcasts could then be conveniently accessed by parents from the school's main Web site.

Going Beyond the School

Parents are a great source of volunteer help, but there are other local resources that can provide additional people power. Look for ways to inform the community about your outdoor learning projects and volunteer needs.

Use Your Web Site

If your school is into outdoor learning, the home page of your Web site should make that known. I am frequently amazed by the number of schools that have excellent outdoor education programs but that haven't publicized this fact on their Web site. Just a picture with a caption referring to outdoor learning can communicate a strong message. Some schools place a link to another page that shows several examples of how the school uses outdoor instruction. The podcasting idea mentioned previously also underscores your interest in using the school grounds as a teaching tool.

Look to Other Area Schools

If you work at an elementary building, consider looking to your local middle school, high school, or vocational/career center for possible volunteer help. One southern school has worked out a partnership with the local high school to have some students come for a workday twice each year. It's amazing how much a well-organized group of teenagers can accomplish in a half-day!

The growing interest in service learning programs for secondary students may also provide teens who are willing to help with a variety of projects. Since vocational centers frequently have specific programs to train students in nature-related occupations, instructors are often looking for projects in the community.

When using students from other schools, I have found the following tips to be helpful:

- Request only small groups (fifteen or fewer). It's too difficult to monitor and keep large groups of students on task.
- Be certain that a staff member from the helping school is present for the entire workday. Things seem to go much better when there is an adult in charge who the students already know and acknowledge as an authority figure.
- Be sure that the helping school knows well in advance what tasks you would like to accomplish. Have a list of specific jobs and provide the necessary materials, such as trash bags, rakes, and so on.
- Be sure that the administration at both your school and the helping school are completely informed about the workday plans. E-mail can provide an efficient way to keep everyone in the loop and can also provide a written record for reference.

Partner with Clubs and Organizations

Community groups are frequently looking for small projects. Garden clubs are an obvious choice, but frequently community service clubs like Kiwanis or Rotary may be willing to take on a project.

Probably the greatest contributors to schoolyard improvement projects are scout troops. Nearly every school that I have visited proudly displays plaques acknowledging the work of community scout troops. Students working on Eagle Scout projects are especially eager to help with the type of short-term, but labor-intensive, projects that are needed to create trails or seating areas. One Georgia school site has fifteen Eagle Scout–produced site enhancements, including trails, benches, a weather station, and numerous teaching/learning areas.

The national Girl Scout organization also offers achievement awards similar to the Eagle Scout program. The Girl Scout Gold Award for girls fourteen to eighteen could easily provide opportunities for developing outdoor learning projects on a school site.

Use Weekly Newspapers

Many smaller communities have weekly newspapers that are usually hungry for local news. If you have a need for certain types of volunteers or donations of specific types of materials, the weekly community newspaper can be a great way to get out the word.

Care and Feeding of Volunteers

It's actually more challenging to maintain a loyal volunteer pool than it is to find the initial group of enthusiastic helpers. Careful attention to schedule options, task variety, and recognition of effort will keep people coming back to help.

Develop a Predictable Schedule

It helps to keep workdays on somewhat of a schedule—for example, the third Saturday of every month or the first Monday from 3:00 p.m. to 5:00 p.m. It helps to use several different days and times since some very willing volunteers may not be available on Saturday mornings, but would be delighted to help on a weekday afternoon. Once you determine who your most reliable volunteers are, you can tailor the schedule to best meet their needs.

Consider Theme Days

The Georgia Wildlife Federation suggests using themes "such as seasons, planting and harvesting to make working in the outdoor classroom feel more like a festival than a chore" (Georgia Wildlife Federation 2004, 19). In keeping with a party atmosphere, provide some light refreshments and consider having some parents or older students help with the care of younger children who may accompany volunteers.

Provide Options

Nobody wants to weed *all* the time. Provide lists of tasks to be accomplished, and let volunteers select tasks they would enjoy. If volunteers notice that one task is being overlooked, some kind soul will step forward.

Acknowledge Volunteers

We all appreciate a thank-you. Find appropriate ways to acknowledge the efforts of your volunteers through certificates, social events, newsletters, school assemblies, and so on. One Ohio school has students raise plants to give to volunteers as a small thank-you gift.

A Few Cautions

A loyal group of volunteers can make seemingly overwhelming outdoor learning projects very doable. Volunteers, though, are not staff members, which requires attention to several important concerns.

Plan to Replace

An inevitable reality of school volunteerism is that your star volunteer will leave. Just as the sun always rises, once children leave a school, the parents always exit. An outdoor program should not be defined by one teacher, nor should the parent volunteer effort be driven by the Herculean efforts of one or two parents.

To maintain continuity, it's essential to groom several parent leaders who have children at various stages of progress through the school. It also is a good idea to divide the volunteer effort into several major segments, such as instructional support, site enhancements, fund-raising, and community volunteers. In doing so, you will have four or five parent leaders rather than just one or two who chair an overall effort.

Working with the Overly Zealous

Occasionally, parents can become so enthusiastic about outdoor learning that the volunteer program takes on a life of its own, sometimes going beyond the needs and objectives of teachers. I know of one situation in which a parent volunteer group had an extremely strong leadership core that generated dozens of great ideas for enhancing the school site. There also was a strong group of followers who worked tirelessly to create gardens, pathways, trails, and learning stations. As you can guess, the situation escalated when the group began installing enhancements without carefully checking with teachers as to what was really needed. The outcome was frustrating for everyone. Parents were upset that teachers weren't using the gardens and learning stations that they had spent hundreds of hours creating, and teachers were feeling pressure to use the site more often just because it was there rather than to meet their instructional needs.

It's always an intricate dance to balance volunteer exuberance with the needs and interests of the organization. Here are a few suggestions that seem to work in most situations:

Responders rather than initiators. In the early stages of forming a volunteer parent committee, stress that the group should see itself as a responder to needs rather than as an initiator of projects. Those are two very different roles. As a responder to needs, the group focuses first on finding out what teachers would like to have on the school site. The result is a much healthier relationship between teachers and volunteers and, more important, the creation of site enhancements that are truly wanted and used. This responder point of view needs to be reinforced whenever there is new leadership in the parent volunteer group.

Surveys. Encourage the volunteer group to survey teachers about the types of site enhancements that they would find most useful. They should ask teachers how the site could be improved as a venue for learning and how the site could be enhanced to teach curriculum objectives. When preparing a survey, they should avoid asking questions that put a teacher on the defensive, such as: "Do you ever take your class outdoors for [then list several activities, like measuring, planting a garden, etc.]?"

Instead, the survey should phrase things in a positive or constructive tone:

What would make it easier for you to use the school site for instruction?

Which of the following site enhancements might be useful to you: [then list several ideas that would be feasible for your school, such as gardens, bird observation blind, field study kits, weather station, etc.]?

It is also useful to ask what factors limit a teacher's use of the outdoors. This question will give the committee an indication of the obstacles that may exist.

Staff representation. Always have a school representative as an official member of the volunteer group. It doesn't have to be the same teacher or administrator at every meeting, but someone from the staff needs to be in the loop at all times.

Review District Volunteer Polices

All districts today have policies and procedures for approving volunteers. Frequently, even volunteers who are not working directly with children need to be approved if they are on the school grounds. Depending on state laws or district policies, volunteers may have to have formal background checks and even fingerprinting. At the very least, a visitor identification badge is routinely required, and registration at the school office upon arrival is a must.

It's important to clarify early on with potential volunteers that there will be security procedures that will have to be met. Most people are very understanding of the need for careful security on a school site and are willing to cooperate, especially if they know in advance what will be involved.

Since most volunteer policies were developed for persons helping inside the building or on a formal field trip, you may need to check how the policy relates to persons who are installing or maintaining site enhancements on the school grounds, especially when school is in session. The small amount of time it takes to verify security policies is well worth the effort.

Formal Parent Involvement Programs

When outdoor learning becomes an established feature of a school, more formal parent involvement programs may be helpful. The two examples that follow illustrate how volunteers can be used to help with both instruction and maintenance.

Volunteer Help in the Classroom

Ford Elementary in Acworth, Georgia, has an Earth Parent program. Parents volunteer to teach an environmental/science lesson five to seven times during the school year. Each teacher is asked to have an Earth Parent. The lessons are correlated to the Georgia Performance Standards and are approved by the classroom teachers. The lessons are carefully planned and scheduled after looking at curriculum maps for the year.

The program is sponsored by the school's parent/teacher/student association and is managed by a volunteer coordinator who does the following:

- Coordinates with administration and staff and gets curriculum maps for the year
- Uses curriculum maps from teachers to put lessons in order and gives an overview of lessons to teachers prior to instruction
- Puts together Earth Parent Packets
- Goes over curriculum maps with Lead Earth Parents
- Trains Lead Earth Parents and Earth Parents
- Coordinates outside training opportunities for Earth Parents, such as outdoor education workshops and local training for Project WET and Project WILD

There is a Lead Earth Parent for each grade level who writes new lessons if necessary, makes copies of lessons for teachers and classroom Earth Parents, and gathers all materials needed for the lessons. All volunteers in the Earth Parent program receive training concerning the objectives of the program as well as information related to outdoor teaching tips, safety procedures, and classroom management.

Although this is a complex volunteer program that has been in place for many years, there are elements that could be adapted on a smaller scale for other schools. For example, having a parent volunteer work with a teacher on outdoor instruction could be very doable. Even if that parent didn't teach a lesson, the parent could be very helpful in maintaining outdoor teaching materials, replenishing supplies, taking care of a designated part of the schoolyard site, and so on. It's always helpful to have another adult along when doing an outdoor activity that has several steps.

Adopt a Spot

Just up the road from Ford Elementary is Frey Elementary School. Frey also has an extensive land lab on its 80-acre site. On the grounds are thirteen outdoor classroom locations in addition to numerous gardens. To keep trails trimmed and learning areas easily accessible on such a large tract of land, it was necessary to assemble an impressive volunteer force. The result was

the Frey FROGS (Friends of Green Spaces). A major FROGS initiative is the Adopt-a-Spot program. According to parent Karan Wood, "Families, classes, businesses and volunteer groups care for one outdoor classroom or one segment of trail all year long on their own schedule. In return, adopters are recognized with a sign and photo, marking their spot" (Wood 2006, 38).

The FROGS Adopt-a-Spot program has an extensive handbook (Frey FROGS 2005) that provides the following:

- Liability waiver forms
- A clear statement of what is expected of the volunteer groups and what the group can expect from the FROGS committee
- Safety considerations
- Specifics about how to care for trails, gardens, and outdoor classrooms
- Resources that are available to volunteers (e.g., tools and storage shed)
- A field guide of plants to avoid, treasure, or remove in the land laboratory
- A map of the entire nature area and profiles of the various outdoor classroom sites highlighting the types of regular maintenance needed in each area
- A report form that makes it easy for groups to report tasks completed and any safety hazards or repair needs they may have noticed

You can see this excellent volunteer handbook online at http://eealliance. org/assets/Documents/Initiatives/freyfrogsadopt-a-spothandbookpdfversion. pdf.

The Adopt-a-Spot program is extremely useful because it divides and defines the responsibilities for maintenance. By taking responsibility for one location, much like the popular adopt-a-roadway cleanup programs, a group can focus on a specific area and take pride in keeping it maintained. Most school grounds are not nearly as extensive or developed as Frey's; however, many schools could benefit from encouraging groups to identify an area on the grounds for maintenance. On a small scale, many schools have families sign up to weed a garden plot for specific weeks during the summer. I have found that the schools that are most successful with maintaining outdoor learning sites have divided the maintenance tasks in ways similar in strategy to the Adopt-a-Spot idea.

Raising Funds

Before you read further in this section, I want to be very clear about one thing: Schoolyard-enhanced learning can take place without spending a dime! Going outside to use various math techniques to estimate the height of the flagpole doesn't require money. Likewise, journaling under a tree on the lawn is another opportunity provided free of charge by your schoolyard.

However, as teachers network and share ideas about outdoor learning, they often generate wish lists. For example, the logs currently used for the teaching/meeting area might be OK, but it would be nice to have a little cash for real tables and seating. Raised garden beds are so convenient and compact, but cash might be needed for building materials and plants.

There are three types of donations needed for site enhancement projects: help, materials, and money. Since the topic of volunteer help has been discussed in some depth, this section will focus on obtaining donations of materials and money.

Donations of materials are often easier to obtain than money. Here are a few suggestions from schools that have been successful in obtaining materials:

Contact local construction firms. Often contractors have extra materials from a job that they are willing to donate. Be specific about the type of materials needed and the quantity. One Ohio school requested "some" mulch, and ended up with a semitrailer turning into the driveway! It is possible to have too much of a good thing.

Publish a wish list of items needed in your school newsletter and your local weekly newspaper. You may want to have people contact you first via e-mail to avoid an overload of a particular item.

Check whether there is a plant rescue group in your community. These are folks who dig up native plants at construction sites and are always looking for homes for displaced vegetation.

Contact local nurseries. One Georgia school worked out an interesting arrangement with a large local nursery company. If a customer mentioned the school, a percentage of the sale was credited to the school. The school could then redeem the amount for plant material or gardening equipment.

Finding financial donors for a project can present more of a challenge. Every teacher and administrator who I interviewed stressed the importance of looking for local financial donors first. Grants through national organizations are certainly always a possibility, but they often involve rather lengthy application forms and a long waiting period before the announcement of the outcome of the application.

Here are a few fund-raising suggestions:

Try an adopt-a-tree/bench program. These are programs in which a tree or bench may be purchased in honor, or in memory, of a person or event (see Figure 1.4). These programs have the potential to generate a substantial amount of income. The key, of course, is frequent promotion of the program through the school newsletter and brochures. It's helpful also to strongly promote these as celebration gifts, not primarily memorials.

Keep the price low enough so folks can participate when, for example, a child or grandchild wins the school spelling bee. Some schools use an option approach: participants can buy a perennial for $25, a tree for $50, or a bench for $150. You need to decide whether your goal is to set prices just high enough to cover the cost of an item or whether you want to have money left over to put into an outdoor learning fund for future use.

Check with the "big box" stores. Many large national chain stores have community participation and benevolence as a part of their yearly budget. In most cases, these grants will not be large and will vary yearly, but any amount helps. Often these stores will provide merchandise instead of monetary awards. It's always helpful to ask for specific items.

Be sure to check with smaller businesses in the community also. As schoolyard habitat author Marilyn Wyzga says, "Remember, you are not begging! You are inviting funders into a partnership that will enhance the lives of local children and the environment" (Wyzga 2001, 20).

Explore grants. Although grants can be a lot of work, the payoff can be significant. Read a grant application very carefully and note the language that is used. One school wanted compost bins but was applying for a grant that asked applicants to "specify how the funds will be used to teach recycling." The teacher writing the grant stated that the funds would be used to demonstrate the recycling of plant vegetation (a.k.a. composting!). Notice how the language of the application form was tossed back in the response. Too often novice grant writers go into beautiful detail about the project they are planning but fail to tie everything back to the language in the instructions.

It's also a good idea to apply for more than one grant at a time. Since decisions regarding funding can take anywhere from a few weeks to nearly a year, it's smart to have several potential options in the mix. If you are extremely lucky and find yourself with several funded grants, you can always expand the project or ask the funder for permission to use the funds for related purposes.

Whether you are looking for donations of materials or money, keep the following in mind:

Be sure that you have necessary administrative approval. Before writing letters to community businesses or organizations, and prior to filing grant applications, always check with your administrators. Since schools need to be cautious not to go to the same donors too often, you need to talk with folks who are knowledgeable about past requests that may have been made for unrelated projects.

Plan how donors will be acknowledged. Although it may seem like a small point, donor recognition needs to be discussed early. If you set a precedent by placing a big sign beside the first tree donated, other donors will expect the same, potentially resulting in a forest of plaques.

In the case of tree or other plant material donations, many schools maintain an attractive book or register in the school office or front hallway that lists donors and the materials given. Avoid placing dozens of recognition plaques around the school grounds. Normal weathering and vandalism can make upkeep a headache.

On the other hand, I do feel that donations of structures or large habitat areas should recognize the donors. Visible recognition of significant donations may

Figure 1.4 This sturdy bench on the beautiful grounds of Wooster High School in Ohio includes recycled materials securely bolted into a concrete pad. Using strong, well-anchored materials discourages vandalism and reduces maintenance issues. The concrete pad is a blessing to mowing crews since it eliminates the need to trim around the individual bench posts. Mowing equipment can easily move right around the pad. Notice the discreet signage on the bench that identifies the donor, honoree, or occasion.

Figure 1.5 Ford Elementary near Atlanta gratefully acknowledged the efforts of a local YMCA. The uplifting quote sets a wonderful tone as students and teachers enter the outdoor classroom.

encourage others to contribute. One North Carolina school recognized the efforts of a group to construct an entire outdoor classroom area by incorporating an inspirational quote as a part of the donor recognition (see Figure 1.5).

Thank-you letters, especially if produced by students, are very meaningful to donors of materials, time, or money. Be sure to find a way to include students in expressing appreciation. They could even write the letters outside!

What If It's Only You?

Most handbooks about planning for outdoor learning assume that a schoolwide or grade-level project is in the works. The starting point for many publications is usually after the large committees are in place and a wide variety of both financial and human resources are available. Very often, however, I meet teachers who are interested in outdoor learning but don't have a big group of colleagues ready to plunge in. In fact, they may be the only ones who are interested in the concept.

That's not really a problem. Engaging outdoor learning activities can be done with a minimum of site enhancement. For example, the typical schoolyard has adequate diversity to supply data for a variety of math lesson applications. To extend a geometry lesson, go outside and find shapes in nature; to teach graphing and data analysis techniques, gather information about the makes and models of vehicles in the parking lot. Creative writing can be inspired by sitting on the lawn on a warm spring afternoon.

Start with a Teaching/Meeting Space

If you are itching to enhance the school site in some way, but don't have much help, I would recommend starting with the development of an outdoor teaching/meeting area. This is simply a gathering place near the school where you begin outdoor activities. It's a home base where you can pass out equipment and give directions. The seating materials that are cheapest and easiest to obtain are logs. Logs are very functional. If used vertically, they provide seating for varying heights (and widths!). Log sections also can be easily rolled to other locations. By creating an outdoor meeting place, you are encouraging yourself to use the outdoors more often. In addition, the convenience of an outdoor learning space may inspire others to give outdoor instruction a try.

If logs or other seating options are not possible, you can always opt for sit-upons (makeshift seats) or stadium cushions. Sit-upons can be made cheaply from large plastic storage bags stuffed with newspaper. Inexpensive clipboards for each child to use outside also help to set a good tone for outdoor teaching. There is something very official and task-oriented about carrying a clipboard. The clipboard provides a low-cost outdoor writing surface as well as a means to prevent papers or other materials from blowing away (Figure 1.6). See Chapter 2 for more information about setting up a teaching/meeting area.

Figure 1.6 Clipboards are easy to carry outside and simple to store in the classroom. Even routine tasks seems to take on a little more significance when a clipboard is involved!

Focus on Small, Low-Maintenance Site Enhancements

Although you may have ten different ideas for enhancing the schoolyard, start with something simple first. You also need to have projects that require little maintenance. Large garden plots are tempting, but the maintenance required may go beyond what you or your students and their parents can provide. Here are a few very simple projects for starters:

Bird feeders. A bird feeder outside of a classroom window is a good start. Kids are fascinated by birds, and feeders can even be homemade. Of course, you have to work out a plan for regularly filling the feeders, but that can be a good lesson in both responsibility and stewardship. Be sure that the feeders are easily accessible so that students can fill them. Remember, other critters like feeders also. Raccoons and squirrels can become regular diners, emptying a feeder in a few hours. In some parts of the country, you may even need to be cautious about really big visitors, like bears!

See Chapter 2 for lots of ideas about how to incorporate birds into outdoor learning.

Figure 1.7 This small container garden is a convenient way to show students the types of plants that are frequently placed on rooftop gardens.

Figure 1.8 An easy way to create several different mini-habitats is to vary mowing patterns. Notice how grass on the right is regularly mowed, and a 4- to 5-foot strip adjacent to it is mowed only a few times a season. On the far left is an unmowed area that demonstrates the process of succession and also provides cover and habitat for a variety of animal life.

Container gardens. Simple container gardens can provide an opportunity to experience the various learning opportunities that stem from gardening. A small container garden is easier to manage than a full-sized, flat-on-the-ground garden, but adequate watering and weeding are still concerns. The container garden shown in Figure 1.7 was designed as a small model to show the types of plants often found on rooftop gardens atop large city buildings in Boston.

Be sure that you have a water source reasonably close to the garden. Rain barrels may provide a limited water source in areas not near a faucet.

Unmowed areas. An unmowed area will quickly attract a variety of plants and small animals and insects. This type of biodiverse site makes for more interesting observations than just studying the mowed lawn. Keep the site rather small and away from the front of the building or a parking lot. Unmowed areas can look a little rough, which can make maintenance staff uneasy. Some folks put up a sign saying "Nature Study Area." Figures 1.8 and 1.9 illustrate how leaving a small area untouched can create impressive diversity.

* * * * * *

Whether it's just you, a trio of teachers, or a schoolwide planning committee, it's important to harness what Cam Collyer of Evergreen calls "let's do something now" energy. People who are excited about outdoor learning want to be doing, not just planning. That initial energy is powerful and needs to be focused. Divide planning into phases so that some immediate goals can be accomplished. Teachers and volunteers need the satisfaction of seeing the abstract concept of outdoor learning translated into bugs and blooms.

Figure 1.9 Probably the most pristine example of a small "unmowed area" on a schoolyard is the tiny island of trees on the grounds of Hope School in Hope, Alaska. This small area is a beautiful miniature of the surrounding countryside.

Spotlight 1
A Dreamkeeper

At Ford Elementary School in Acworth, Georgia, Catherine Padgett has become a dreamkeeper. Put simply, her dream is to provide children with rich possibilities for outdoor learning. Both Catherine's story and the Ford Elementary outdoor learning program provide inspiration and practical suggestions for anyone interested in fostering outdoor education.

Meet Catherine Padgett

Like many passionate outdoor educators, Catherine traces her love of the outdoors to childhood experiences. She grew up on a small cattle ranch in southern Mississippi and was greatly influenced by parents and grandparents who loved the land. Nature has always been a part of her life, and a love of the outdoors is a legacy that she wants to pass on. Catherine also is a deeply spiritual person who "sees God's handiwork in nature." Her strong stewardship ethic is framed by the belief that "children will care for what they are knowledgeable and passionate about." Beyond knowledge and passion, though, she feels that students need to be empowered to actively care for their schoolyard environment.

Catherine jokes that she got into education by default. Her college career began with a major in horticulture. Because of a move, however, she found herself at a university that didn't offer a horticulture degree. Since she also had a strong interest in teaching, Catherine changed her major to education and was able to weave her love of plants and gardening into her new career path.

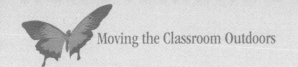

When she took her first teaching job in a small private school in Mississippi, she just opened the classroom door and took children outside. She hadn't attended any outdoor learning workshops or read a book about the value of outdoor education. For her, the idea of incorporating nature into teaching was instinctive.

In 1993 Catherine moved to Acworth, Georgia, and began to teach kindergarten at Ford Elementary. She immediately planted a small 4-by-4-foot garden plot near her classroom and used that as a teaching tool. Soon Catherine wanted to expand the outdoor garden area. Her principal agreed, set aside an unused strip of land at the side of the school, and gave her $200 for materials. That initial gesture of confidence encouraged Catherine to begin a mission that continues to this day.

Seeing the need for more funding, Catherine spoke to community groups and knocked on the doors of local businesses to increase available funds. As she looked for funding sources, Catherine discovered a $5,000 grant offered by the *Atlanta Journal-Constitution*. By writing and being awarded her first-ever grant, Catherine received not only funding but also strong encouragement to move ahead with plans for schoolyard enhancement.

A small environmental design team of teachers was formed to encourage outdoor learning and to plan future projects. The team encouraged colleagues to try some outdoor teaching by adopting a "spot, pot, or plot." The school, however, was facing tremendous challenges. Rapid population growth in this suburban Atlanta community caused enrollment to swell to 2,000 students in a building originally intended for under 1,000. The overcrowded conditions spawned the construction of two additional elementary buildings in the community.

The grant Catherine had received posed a bit of a dilemma. It had been written for one school of 2,000 students, but now there were three schools. Although Catherine stayed at Ford, she sent $1,000 to each of the two new schools as seed money to start outdoor projects at these locations. She wanted to be sure that the students leaving Ford had an opportunity to enter a new building that had some seed money for outdoor learning.

Today Ford Elementary houses about 900 students in grades Pre-K–5 and is located on approximately twenty acres of land that includes a wooded buffer on all sides. Ford is a part of the Cobb County School District, the second largest school system in Georgia, serving more than 107,000 students in 114 schools.

Innovative Features

A sincere interest in outdoor learning at Ford Elementary spawned several programs, activities, and site enhancements that could inspire other teachers and schools. It's important to keep in perspective, however, that these features have been initiated, cultivated, and refined over a period of nearly two decades. Outdoor learning at Ford provides inspiring examples of steady and sustained effort over time.

Earth Parent Program

This well-planned and long-lasting program is explained in more detail in Chapter 1. The enthusiasm of parent volunteers has done much to sustain the Ford outdoor education efforts for over fifteen years. One parent per classroom is trained to teach five to seven environmental/ science lessons each school year, in consultation with the classroom teacher. This strong involvement of parents builds both an understanding of the value of outdoor learning as well as a strong pride in the school's outdoor site enhancements. For teachers, the parent program provides an occasional change of pace and place in the classroom while still focusing on the academic curriculum.

Evening in the Garden

Although Ford has many valuable programs and initiatives in place, Evening in the Garden has probably had the greatest impact upon the sustainability of outdoor learning at the building. This unique May event is billed as a celebration of the arts and environmental programs at Ford. Art and music teachers play a pivotal role in producing this marvelous event, which blends together displays of student artwork, an outdoor multigrade musical performance, student presentations of creative writing, and individual student musical performances.

All of this is done with a "picnic in the park" feel, showcasing the gardens that have been nurtured by the various classrooms in the building. It is a unique blending of the arts with the efforts that have been put into the gardens. Since this is a school wide event that encompasses several disciplines it has the support of many people. Although Catherine coordinates much of the planning, all grade levels are actively involved.

As you walk around the perimeter of the school building, you may encounter a student musician playing the

Parents, students, and school staff join for an evening that spotlights both student creativity and the inspiring outdoor learning environment at Ford.

piano or a young violinist demonstrating her talent in a garden that was planted and cared for by her classmates. Since the evening event has been in place now for more than a decade, former students will often return to perform at Evening in the Garden, adding both pride and nostalgia to the event. Side venues are also used and include such backdrops as a wooded teaching area where students read original poems to proud parents and friends seated in the outdoor classroom.

The event also serves as a fund-raiser for the outdoor learning program. Although families are welcome to bring their own picnic meals, there also is an option to purchase food, soft drinks, and desserts.

This wonderful event builds highly supportive parent and community relations. Because the entire student body is involved in one way or another, parents who wouldn't normally visit the school have an opportunity to stroll through the grounds and see the variety of venues dedicated to outdoor learning. Even classroom windows display student work, often inspired by an outdoor activity. Since the displays are visible from the outside, parents are treated to a showcase of student work and see how the outdoor experiences are incorporated in the classroom. It's like a traditional school open house, but everyone is outside looking in!

Site Enhancements

When new schools were constructed, modular units were removed from the Ford Elementary site, leaving behind an eroded area. Catherine's answer was to start an adopt-a-tree program,

which allowed donors to give trees or shrubs in honor or in memory of an individual. The result was 125 trees and shrubs that have filled in eroded areas. Many of the donated trees became a hillside arboretum leading to the school playground.

Ford incorporates an amazing number of outdoor learning venues. A variety of themed gardens are located immediately outside of the building to facilitate easy access and serendipitous instructional opportunities. Some gardens are based on books children have read, while another is a sensory garden that emphasizes plants with unusual colors, textures, and fragrances and includes small wind chimes to create relaxing sounds.

In addition to highly accessible gardens, the school also has a hillside amphitheater between the

This garden incorporates some plants mentioned in books children have read in class.

school and the playground. Several additional outdoor learning areas have been constructed on the site, including a "woods classroom" that is less than a hundred yards from the building but creates a wonderful feeling of being in a forest. Another outdoor teaching/meeting platform has been constructed right outside a side door. The site even has a nature trail for teachers wanting to do a traditional hiking experience with their students. Fifteen Eagle Scout projects have contributed greatly to the creation of these site enhancements.

Sustainability

To keep a program going at such a complex and multidimensional level for more than sixteen years is truly amazing. Currently, Catherine is working for her fifth administrator at Ford. Former principal Peggy Pepper credits the high level of respect with which Catherine is regarded by her colleagues as a major factor in maintaining the program. In addition, Catherine's infectious enthusiasm just naturally encourages collegial and parental involvement in maintaining the outdoor learning program.

Around one side of the building is a Georgia native plant garden that showcases the variety of plants growing in various regions of the state.

The Ford Elementary School Foundation was established in 2005 to receive donations from the community. A recent focus of the foundation has been the establishment of a science lab at Ford that is staffed by a science specialist.

Catherine emphasizes that the empowerment of peers, community, and students is essential. That empowerment comes from creating teacher-friendly, safe, and easily accessible sites. National outdoor learning programs like Project Learning Tree and Project WILD have been brought to the school to provide teachers with additional ideas for using the outdoors. Catherine says it well: "If people only talk of *your* garden, then people are not empowered." She says that her biggest learning over the years has been this: "When you don't delegate, you don't empower."

Without a doubt, Catherine Padgett is a dreamkeeper. She has nurtured, cajoled, begged, and sweated to make and maintain outdoor learning as a part of her school. Her love of nature and confidence in its power to teach and heal has never wavered. After Hurricane Katrina, Ford

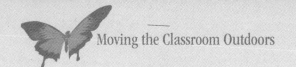

sent two tractor trailers of school supplies and other materials to the devastated area in a "Tubs of Love" program. But Catherine wanted to do something herself. In her own words, "The only thing I knew to do was to load up my truck with planters and plants." Her contribution to those in need was to try to restore a few spots of beauty—to encourage others to become dreamkeepers in the midst of devastation.

Chapter 2
Enhancing the Schoolyard for Outdoor Learning

Over the past twenty years, there has been a growing interest in making the schoolyard more functional and appealing. Many early efforts focused almost entirely on the installation of play equipment that offered more variety than the traditional swings and sliding boards. Slowly, emphasis has been turning to thoughts about how to use the school grounds not only for recreation but also to enhance instruction. Our steadily increasing societal interest in the environment coupled with uneasiness about the amount of time students spend video-vegetating indoors has made schoolyard-enhanced learning an intriguing option.

One Ohio principal uses the term *infrastructure* to describe the enhancements that are made to school grounds to create a more teacher- and learner-friendly outdoor instructional environment. Bird blinds, raised garden beds, or outdoor seating areas can indeed be viewed as underlying features that create a framework for effective outdoor teaching. Although you certainly can teach outdoors using only the vegetation that grows through sidewalk cracks, instructional options increase dramatically when there are designated learning areas, plantings, and conveniences as part of the schoolyard learning infrastructure.

This chapter provides dozens of options for enhancing outdoor learning environments. I owe a huge thank-you to more than sixty teachers, administrators, and designers from the United States and Canada who shared their best

ideas and practical tips for schoolyard enhancement. Since a picture can often convey more than a long paragraph, an abundant collection of images has been assembled to help you visualize how enhancements might look on your site.

Some Basic Vocabulary

To avoid confusion, let's clarify a few terms. *Schoolyard greening* is rapidly becoming the common term for adding elements to the schoolyard that make it a place for active and interactive play and learning. A Google search using "schoolyard greening" generates more than four thousand hits. The term usually refers to both the utilization of more natural play elements and the addition of learning elements such as gardens or unmowed areas. The term *schoolyard transformation* is sometimes used synonymously with *greening*, especially in Canada.

I use the term *schoolyard enhancement* to refer to both natural elements and man-made features that are added to a school site for *the express purpose of facilitating instruction*. Careful thought is given in advance as to how the elements will mesh with the curriculum and the instructional needs of teachers. Bird feeders, outdoor teaching/meeting areas, trails, sundials, garden plots, and so on all would be considered schoolyard enhancements if they have been added primarily to provide instructional options or venues.

It's important to make a distinction between beautification projects and schoolyard enhancement. Beautification projects certainly do lift everyone's spirits, and they can even provide learning if students are part of the planning and installation process. But if a project is primarily being done to make things look better, with little intent to incorporate it into regular instruction, then it really wouldn't be considered schoolyard learning enhancement. We all have seen schools that are beautifully landscaped but where children rarely go outside to interact with the natural elements as part of a lesson.

Now please don't misunderstand—I'm not opposed to outdoor beautification projects! An attractive, well-maintained school site communicates a sense of pride and creates a welcoming atmosphere. Indeed, many outdoor instructional enhancements can serve both as teaching resources and as touches of beauty. School garden plots and educational plantings can very easily work at both levels. On the other hand, some instructional enhancements, such as unmowed areas and animal tracking pits, aren't really pretty and might be better placed behind the building rather than in front.

The term *outdoor classroom* can take on a variety of meanings. For some schools it is a small, clearly defined space that includes carefully arranged natural materials selected according to the curriculum. As is discussed in Chapter 4, many urban schools out of necessity need to develop compact learning areas on small school sites. For schools on larger tracts of land, the outdoor classroom frequently is made up of several learning venues. The following sections describe these venues.

Outdoor Teaching/Meeting Area

Whether the site is small or large, it is essential to provide an outdoor teaching/meeting space. I strongly advise those interested in starting an outdoor learning initiative to begin by first locating a suitable staging area near the school.

The outdoor teaching/meeting area is more than just a location—it's a powerful classroom management tool. Rather than just running out the door and scattering on the lawn, students know that they are to move directly to the meeting area, where they will sit, hear directions for the activity, and receive materials—actually experience an introduction to a lesson just as they would indoors. Since many teachers mention management concerns as a primary reason for hesitating to go outdoors, it is prudent to develop the meeting area first.

A few essential considerations to keep in mind when developing a teaching/meeting area are described in the following sections.

Keep It Close to the Building

The less walking time, the better. The longer the walk to the teaching/meeting area, the longer it will take to bring everyone back on task. If you plan to work in a location that is away from the building, you should still begin in a teaching/meeting area close to the school, where you will explain the activity and your expectations, and then move to the actual site. Figures 2.1 through 2.5 show some of the many options for teaching/meeting areas.

Figure **2.1** This very simple teaching/meeting site includes two picnic-style tables located right at the bottom of the stairs leading from the building. Nothing fancy, but students can get to work immediately upon leaving the classroom.

Figure 2.2 This is a more elaborate outdoor seating area, but it also is located very near the classroom. The benches are movable and a basic table is provided for the organization of supplies.

Figure 2.3 Here is a wonderful example of a cozy little outdoor teaching/meeting area located at the corner of a building. Although benches are used here, logs would work just fine.

Figure 2.4 This meeting space is as close to the building as you can possibly be! The perimeter of the building is prepared for planting, so students are literally in the midst of their work. The location of a water faucet on the building wall is a great bonus.

Figure 2.5 Here is the simplest and most unobtrusive meeting area possible—just a long bench. The bench serves as a good beginning point for explaining directions and beginning outdoor activities.

Give Careful Thought to Seating

After you have determined where the teaching/meeting area will be located, the next decision is seating. It's important to keep in mind that an outdoor learning space is not an outdoor lecture hall—hopefully, students will be spending a minimum amount of time sitting and listening and a maximum amount of time moving and exploring. Although seating should not be obviously uncomfortable, it also does not need to simulate indoor classroom furniture.

Consider using inexpensive materials, such as logs, stone blocks, or large rocks. You can always buy more permanent seating later once you are sure where you will spend the most time.

Keep seats in close proximity. Too often schools want to build amphitheater-style seating as the first project and then plan to use that as the teaching/meeting area. Tiered amphitheater-style seats such as those shown in Figure 2.6 provide fine performance venues but usually do not work well as outdoor classroom staging areas. Students are too spread out, and tiered seating is just not conducive to discussions. The following sections describe seating options in more detail.

Logs as Seating

Logs are ideal seating material. They are inexpensive or free, very easily obtained, and readily moved. Logs placed vertically will accommodate varying student heights, and, by including several log diameters, most any size posterior can also be accommodated.

Logs also can capture the history of a site. At one North Carolina school, a large tree had provided shade and a reading area for many years. After it came down during a storm, teacher Sally Massengale asked to have the logs saved to create an outdoor seating area (see Figures 2.7a–b).

Since logs are so portable, they can be used most anywhere (Figure 2.8). Logs also work well when placed horizontally (Figure 2.9). And, finally, interest can be added to log seating areas by including the unusual or unexpected (Figure 2.10).

A few thoughts about logs as seating: Probably the major downside to using logs is that they are destined to disappear! Especially

Figure 2.6 This amphitheater-style teaching/meeting area is certainly attractive and useful but is better suited for watching a program than launching a lesson.

Figure 2.7a Former branches of an old tree become functional seating.

Figure 2.7b The stump of the old tree remains near its former branches and provides a good discussion starter.

Figure 2.8 The trailside location of this log seating area is moved as the seasons change and different areas of interest are highlighted.

Figure 2.9 As shown here, when logs are placed horizontally, it's possible to get a little more seating out of a section of log. The only downside is that all students are seated at the same rather low height.

Figure 2.10 This outdoor storytelling area at the North Carolina Botanical Garden in Chapel Hill is made very special by the inclusion of a unique reader's "chair."

in damp areas, logs will rot in a few years and will need to be replaced. Contact a local nature center to learn what types of trees are most rot resistant in your area. Some teachers have also noted that logs may attract nests of insects, so it's a good policy to inspect and replace logs as needed.

Although replacement will be necessary, a rotting log beautifully turns into a teaching tool when its useful life as a seat is over. Just lay the log on its side near your outdoor learning area and let students watch how the log becomes a habitat for tiny critters and eventually enriches the soil.

Rocks and Boulders as Seating

Rocks and boulders are not as portable as logs, but they can also provide very functional seating options (Figure 2.11). One southern school turned a boulder field adjoining the school grounds into a teaching/meeting area (Figure 2.12).

Rocks and stones are certainly durable, but they're also heavy. Before installing a rock or boulder seating area, you need to be very sure that your location will not need to be changed.

Figure 2.11 This innovative teaching/meeting area at a Boston school mixes log, boulder, and low wall seating in several different configurations.

Figure 2.12 Kids are delighted to scramble on the rocks to find a seat in this teaching/meeting area. Some benches are provided for those who might not want to be rock climbers.

Another potential downside of rock seating is the difficulty of trimming around the rocks if they are in a grassy area. Logs can be easily rolled aside for mowing, but rocks require manual trimming or their surroundings can look overgrown by midsummer. Provide frequent thanks (and occasional doughnuts!) to maintenance personnel if you are placing rocks in an area that is usually mowed.

A Few Other Inexpensive Options

Wisconsin science teacher Matt Tiller constructed some unique and easy-to-make portable outdoor seating (Figure 2.13a–b). He credits Verona Area High School colleague Hope Mikkelson with the original design. The seats are wide enough for easy sitting, keep students off the wet ground, and are

Figure 2.13a Using colleague Hope Mikkelson's design, science teacher Matt Tiller constructed several small platform seats.

Figure 2.13b The seats are supported by two-by-eights. Three 24-inch-long one-by-four planks are set side by side to form the seats. A two-by-four runs between the two-by-eights to provide stability.

very portable. The length is also adequate for students to sit and place their journals on the platform for writing. These small platforms can be carried easily from place to place and don't take up much room in a storage area. Since they can be easily stored, the platforms are not continually exposed to the weather, which extends their usefulness and does not require the use of treated wood.

Figure 2.14 Here, cable spools and logs are used together so students have both seats and tables to write on.

Cable spools provide another inexpensive seating option (Figure 2.14). They come in a variety of sizes and are usually free. Power companies and cable TV providers are usually willing to give these items to schools. Spools can serve dual purposes in your teaching/meeting area. Small spools can serve as seats, and larger spools function quite nicely as tables.

Cable spools, however, are not manufactured for long-term outdoor use. They also are not designed for use with children. Carefully check spools for exposed nails, splinters, and rough edges. To prolong the life of the spools, many teachers apply a few coats of paint.

A caution about cable spools: Although cable spools can be easily rolled from place to place, their large, awkward size can make indoor storage very difficult—that's why companies gladly give them away! Also, as the spools deteriorate, their size and weight can create a challenge for disposal as well as an eyesore.

Figure 2.15 This simple seating area is close to the building but away from the walkways and play areas. Note how even a few trees can soften the site and provide a little shade.

Be Aware of Distractions and Student Traffic Patterns

Keep the teaching/meeting area away from nearby playground equipment and walking routes that students and adults typically use when going to and from the building (Figure 2.15). You don't need to be isolated, but you also don't want to be frequently interrupted by classes going to recess or visitors going to and from the building.

Be Aware of Sun and Shade

Depending on where you live, the need for shade may or may not be an important consideration. If you know there will be a certain time of day when the space will get heavy usage, try to find a spot that may be a bit sheltered from the sun at that time. Although not essential, some type of sun shelter can be very useful, especially in very sunny climates or on schoolyards that have no trees.

One Ohio school recently constructed a sun shelter that will eventually serve as an arbor for climbing vines that will provide both shade and interest (Figure 2.16a–b). On a smaller scale, a Georgia school constructed an arbor with a vine that is nearly as old as the building (Figure 2.17).

Figure 2.16a A view of the arbor from the side. A worktable is provided, and a mix of both long and short bench seating is included.

Figure 2.16b A view of the arbor from within.

If funding is available, a pavilion can serve as a multipurpose space that provides protection from both sun and rain (Figure 2.18). A popular variation on the pavilion concept is a gazebo (Figure 2.19). A gazebo provides an attractive visual element to a site and creates the sense of a "special place" that is hard to duplicate with a pavilion. Pavilions, however, do provide options for holding many other school events, such as picnics, and can often provide more roof coverage for the same price. If pavilion seating is not fixed, the area can be cleared or rearranged for a variety of functions.

Figure 2.17 This great little space is close to the building, incorporates plant material, and provides intimate seating that is perfect for reading a story or having a discussion.

Figure 2.18 This large pavilion has easy access from all sides and provides a solid floor for additional work space and easy cleanup.

Figure 2.19 Worth County Primary School in Sylvester, Georgia, has lush garden and arbor areas that lead naturally to an inviting gazebo. What a wonderful spot to begin or end an outdoor activity!

When structural elements such as large arbors, gazebos, or pavilions are added to a site, it's essential to check into local building codes and insurance regulations. Often, there are very rigid specifications that must be met when constructing elements to be used with children.

Although it's tempting to look immediately for donations to build a nifty gazebo or a pavilion that will hold fifty kids, I recommend that schools put that type of project into the long-term goals file. Develop your outdoor classroom spaces first with inexpensive, easily moved elements like logs or simple benches. Next, enhance the site by providing a diversity of plant life and animal habitats. After a few years, as usage patterns begin to emerge, you can re-evaluate whether more formal meeting areas like pavilions or gazebos would be helpful. As time goes by, it also becomes more obvious where permanent structures should be placed for maximum usage.

Provide for Special Needs

The outdoor teaching/meeting area must be easily accessible to students with special needs in your building. Early in the planning stage, look at your school population and think about the types of accommodations that need to be made in the teaching/meeting area as well as in access routes to the outdoor classroom. Attention to these details makes it possible for every child to access the teaching/meeting area (see Figures 2.20 and 2.21).

Figure 2.20 This picnic table is specially designed to accommodate wheelchairs.

Figure 2.21 This pathway is made from a stabilized slate material that provides a level and relatively smooth surface for those needing mobility assistance. Planners also designed the pathway to be wide enough for a golf cart.

Site Enhancements for the Outdoor Classroom

Establishing a teaching/meeting area is the first step in developing an outdoor classroom. Remember that many outdoor learning activities can be done immediately using nothing more than the school lawn and the trees and vegetation that already exist on the site. However, there are many enhancements that can be added to the school grounds to make the site an even more versatile and engaging resource. In this section we look at examples of plantings, pathways, signage, and entrances, as well as other interesting instructional elements that can be added to a site.

Planting with a Purpose

Without a doubt, the most common schoolyard enhancements that I have seen are gardens of one sort or another. They sometimes are quite formal, with pathways and unique entrances, while others are really just plants clustered on the grounds for a specific purpose. Plantings that are used for schoolyard enhancement usually fall into one of these categories:

Plantings related to curricular concepts. For example, one Ohio family and consumer science teacher has her students plant herbs for use during a foods unit. A North Carolina teacher uses a garden to help her first graders explore the five senses. She includes plants that have interesting

textures, smells, shapes and colors, and tastes (mint is used for this one). Ornamental grasses and wind chimes provide sounds to complete the sensory experience. A Georgia teacher has a garden that includes the flowers and plants mentioned in several children's books.

Plantings related to the regional economy or history. A good example is the Three Sisters Garden, which is grown to demonstrate the three main agricultural crops of many Native American groups. The function and arrangement of beans, squash, and corn provides a fascinating history lesson as well as insight into agricultural practices and nutrition. The three plants grow well in most areas of the United States and Canada.

Plants associated with the local economy, such as cotton, are often incorporated into school plantings. One Ohio teacher plants state flowers for her state and all of the states contiguous to Ohio.

Plantings that create a habitat for wildlife. Although they often do not resemble traditional gardens, the planting of trees and shrubs on the school grounds provides cover and food sources for wildlife. Schools often plant rather formal butterfly gardens, but a bush planted near a classroom window can also encourage critters to come a little closer.

Plantings to honor or remember. Many schools have commemorative gardens or groves that recognize special people, events, or achievements. Frequently, these special areas have benches or winding pathways to promote a sense of reflection.

Planting Options

The type of planting that you choose is determined by several factors:

- Amount of available space
- Types of plants appropriate for your climate and topography
- Maintenance concerns and the availability of volunteer help

This section provides an overview of many styles and approaches to plantings in the schoolyard. There are really only two major options for the first stage of planting: (1) choose a location and till a plot of soil or (2) install some type of raised bed or container garden. Although I see both types in my visits to schools, raised gardens seem to be the most popular choice on school grounds.

Raised gardens do have many advantages. Because you don't walk within a raised garden, you avoid the problems of soil compaction that occur in a traditional flat garden. Penn State professor Dr. Michael Orzolek points out that "plants in raised beds get more sun and air circulation, and they can make better use of water. You often can plant earlier and harvest later, because raised beds warm up early in the spring and stay warm later in the fall" (1995, 1).

Penn State's Agricultural Information Service emphasizes that the garden frame for raised beds needs to be constructed of nontoxic material, such as "stone, cinder blocks, bricks, untreated wood, or fiberglass." The service also advises: "Avoid pressure-treated lumber and creosote-treated railroad ties." The recommendation is that a frame twelve to sixteen inches high is used. To keep the bed sturdy, boards "must be secured at the corners with metal braces or screws, or nailed to a reinforcing block of wood inside the corners—if you nail into the ends of boards, they will split" (Orzolek 1995, 2).

Raised beds can be easier for students to manage, since many people can stand around the bed to plant or weed. In addition, raised beds provide wonderful access for students in wheelchairs.

Figures 2.22 through 2.26 show some examples of convenient and efficient raised beds.

Figure 2.22 These basic raised beds are placed near the school for quick access. The L shape provides an interesting visual variation as well as a way to separate plantings.

Figure 2.22 This Georgia school has raised beds for most every classroom. As with successful teaching/meeting areas, it is in close proximity to the school. The pavilion in the background is used as an outdoor teaching/meeting area.

Figure 2.24 This Ohio school has raised beds located directly outside of the classroom tending the plantings.

Figure 2.25 Ford Elementary in Georgia has taken the idea of a flower "bed" literally. The clever ornamental headboard and footboard add a whimsical feel to these storybook garden beds.

Figure 2.26 The addition of a simple visual element makes this flat garden a focal point.

Figure 2.27 These raised gardens are on the grounds of a school in the small town of Hope, Alaska. The tall fence is to deter both rabbits and moose!

Community Gardens

The increasing popularity of homegrown produce has led to an interest in local gardening. Schools with adequate open space can provide an ideal location for community gardens. Although community gardens like the one pictured in Figure 2.27 are not school projects, they add an interesting feature to the school site and help to foster good school/community relations.

Most community gardens are organized by a local group external to the school. When opening the school grounds to the community, it is essential that the school has a contact person who can handle communications with the gardeners and will enforce school expectations and regulations.

To avoid misunderstandings, a written list of expectations and usage rules needs to be developed jointly by the contact person and the school district administration. For example, trash removal, safe storage of equipment, watering arrangements, trimming around the garden site, acceptable times for working when school is in session, and end-of-season cleanup of the site are just a few of the items that need to be spelled out before community gardening begins on a school site. Maintenance of the community garden needs to rest with the sponsoring organization. School maintenance staff should not be expected to oversee the site or clean up the area after the growing season.

The most successful community gardens on school sites are those sponsored by a recognized community organization after careful discussion and the development of a written agreement. Frequently, community gardens inspire teachers to try a classroom garden the next season!

Pathways

Pathways direct activity and add structure to an outdoor classroom. They guide footsteps away from certain areas or materials and can call attention to features that might otherwise be missed. Pathways can be as simple as mulch or wood chips, or as intricate as imprinted concrete or student-produced stepping-stones.

Basic Pathway Materials

The most basic pathways use mulch or wood chips to delineate a route and keep weeds down. Although not essential, the use of outline material helps to keep kids from straying off the trail. It's possible to create functional and beautiful pathways with simple materials, but even when using materials such as concrete, it's possible to add a unique touch. It's important to take into account practical considerations, such as access for maintenance staff, when planning pathways.

By imbedding impressions of plants near a sidewalk, an instant teaching and awareness building tool is created. Some schools create sidewalks with impressions of natural materials that students have found anywhere on the site. Students enjoy selecting materials to include and in the process are taking a closer look at their natural surroundings. Figures 2.28 through 2.35 depict some of the striking, yet useful, pathways I've encountered in my school visits.

Figure 2.28 This pathway uses rocks to outline the general route, with wood chips providing the surface material.

Figure 2.29 This photo shows a wood chip trail that uses logs instead of rocks to outline the route.

Figure 2.30 Rails delineate the path on this trail, but an opening has been left so that mowing equipment can easily enter the lawn to the left. Adding little details like this help to make the maintenance staff feel a part of your project.

Figure 2.31 Boulders and crushed stone create a path that blends beautifully with its surroundings. This path actually leads to the front of the school building.

Figure 2.32 This path in a Boston schoolyard gently guides children through the area by using boulders, logs, and plants as the pathway markers.

Figure 2.33a–b These photos show what can be done to add a little flair to a path. The use of pavers or wooden planks would be too expensive for a long path, but materials like these can add a neat accent to highlight a special area.

Figure 2.34 To help finance a project, some schools accept donations for inscribed bricks in the pathway.

Figure 2.35a A school in Georgia took advantage of a new concrete sidewalk that was being poured. The sidewalk went through an area that had plants representing meadow vegetation, so the words "meadow walk" were scratched in the concrete.

Figure 2.35b Concrete impressions were made of typical plants and animal tracks that might be found in a meadow.

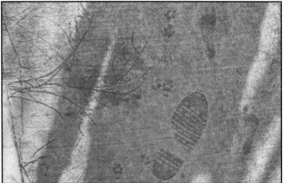

Figure 2.35c Human footprints provide a whimsical touch that gives the walk a personal feel.

Incorporating Stepping-Stones

Using stepping-stones in pathways is far less expensive than pouring concrete walkways. I'm a real fan of stepping-stones because they provide versatility, functionality, and an opportunity for student creativity. Stepping-stones can keep feet dry in wet conditions, cut down on the amount of dirt or mulch tracked into the building, and provide wonderful focal points and discussion starters. Because stepping-stones are easy to make and simple to replace, they can be easily exchanged as seasons progress or as a new unit of study begins.

Stepping-stone kits can be purchased at craft stores, but if you are willing to assemble materials yourself, you can make stones for a fraction of the kit price. A Google search using the phrase "making garden stepping-stones" will

Figure 2.36a Students at a Georgia school were invited to bring in interesting natural items to put in the stepping-stones.

Figure 2.36b Rocks, bits of wood, and pieces of shell were pressed into the cement to form these stepping-stones.

yield dozens of creative and practical ideas for making stones yourself. See Figures 2.36a and b and 2.37 for examples.

Sarah Palmer teaches at the Wiley International Magnet School in Raleigh, North Carolina. She encouraged her colleagues to provide stepping-stones for their outdoor study area that would coordinate with the international theme of the school. Figures 2.38 and 2.39 show the results, and Figures 2.40 through 2.42 depict a few other stepping-stone pathways.

Figure 2.37 This clever set of stepping-stones was inspired by Eric Carle's book *The Very Hungry Caterpillar.*

Figure 2.38 Some classes elected to make stones that represented a particular country.

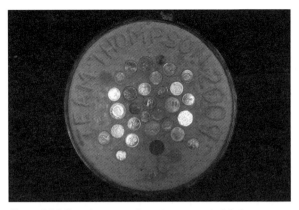

Figure 2.39 One classroom chose to represent global awareness by having students bring in coins from other countries. The coins were then incorporated into a stepping-stone!

Figure 2.40 Even flat pieces of stone work well for a pathway. The randomly arranged slabs of stone in this Boston outdoor classroom give a welcoming feel to the area.

Figure 2.41 Stone pieces are used effectively at one Ohio school to create a contrast in this garden area at the side of the building.

Figure 2.42 Commercial stepping-stones provide an interesting look to this area on a Georgia school site.

Signage

My preference is to keep signage unobtrusive, minimal, and purposeful. Too often natural areas are visually littered with extensive signage that actually competes with the natural features it seeks to describe. On the other hand, carefully planned labels, markers, and occasional information boards or kiosks can be very helpful.

If you have a nature trail on your site, consider using small numbered markers to indicate points of interest. There are several reasons why I prefer numbered marking systems over the more traditional detailed interpretive trail signs that give names, pictures, and natural history information:

- Numbering systems allow you to readily change the placement of a point of interest without having to incur the cost of a new sign—you only have to change the printed sheet that explains the numbers.
- Although not vandal proof, a small number sign is less likely to be disturbed and is much easier to replace than larger text signage.
- Numbered markers are much less expensive than weather-resistant interpretive panels.
- With numbered points of interest, students can write the descriptions themselves. Indeed, the development of the guide can turn into a learning activity. See Chapter 1 for more about student-written nature guides.

As you peruse the signage shown in Figures 2.43 through 2.47, consider the ways you can design and implement your signage economically, with student involvement when possible, and so that the signage serves a practical purpose without being obtrusive.

Figure 2.43a–b Here are two examples of numerical trail signage. The most inexpensive is the hand-numbered PVC pipe. The numbered locations are referenced in a printed handout that students use on the trail.

One last thought about signage. Probably one of the simplest, yet most dynamic, enhancements to a schoolyard is to designate an area that is permitted to return to a natural state. That, of course, is synonymous with long grass, straggly vines, and scrub trees.

Figure 2.44 Another inexpensive signage option is the small plant identification tags used by greenhouses, as shown here.

Figure 2.45 Students can produce signs like this one using a classroom computer after researching information about the nature object to be highlighted. The student-made sign is then laminated and attached to a backing board with plastic clips. This is a great way for students to feel a part of trail interpretation with signs that can be easily and inexpensively changed on a regular basis.

Figure 2.46 This entrance sign for a nature trail at the Susan B. English School in Seldovia, Alaska, clearly sums up the effort that was involved in creating the magnificent trail that winds through a temperate rain forest adjoining the school grounds. The sign starts your hike with a chuckle but also is a tribute to the volunteer effort that was required. A nice feature at the end of this trail are laminated signs that give a little history of the trail and list the names of all those who helped with the project. The trail name, Otterbahn, was inspired by the school's mascot—the otter.

Figure 2.47a–b A teacher in Chapel Hill, North Carolina, has students make wonderful plant identification signs as art projects. Students write and draw descriptions on small clay tiles. The tiles are then glazed and fired to form weatherproof signage that is also inexpensive and easily changed.

Our culture, however, often expects to see neatly mowed school grounds. A simple sign that tells people that this is an outdoor study site or a research area works beautifully and makes it clear that the area isn't being ignored (see Figure 2.48). Rather, it's a part of a noble effort!

Figure 2.48 This sign reassures people that the area is not being neglected but is part of the educational program.

Entrances

Entrances to outdoor learning areas set an important tone. They invite students and visitors into the outdoor space and convey that the space has a special

purpose. As you'll see in Figures 2.49 through 2.52, the materials and designs used in entrances can hold special meaning and create a variety of visual effects.

Although an outdoor bulletin board is relatively expensive, it could be a long-term goal for the site; or, it could become a part of an Eagle Scout project. Bulletin boards like the one shown in Figure 2.53 are especially useful for trails that are frequently used by both neighborhood residents and students. Bulletin boards can provide a number of functions:

Figure 2.49 The addition of a simple decorative fence with plantings invites the learner into this outdoor learning space at a Wisconsin school. Without the fence, the area would not have nearly the same appeal.

Figure 2.50a–b This outdoor classroom site at Ford Elementary in Acworth, Georgia, has a decorative railing designed by a local artist. If you look carefully at the railing, you'll see that none of the decorative spindles are exactly the same, symbolizing that every child is unique. What a marvelous lesson being communicated in an entrance!

- Gallery of student work that has been done on the outdoor site
- Information about the plants and animals found on the site
- Map and directional information
- Rules or expectations regarding site usage (this is a good place to specify that the trail is closed from dusk to dawn, for example)
- List of donors (both financial and in-kind) who have contributed to outdoor learning at the school
- Information about coming events, such as a plant sale
- Phone numbers or other contact information to report problems that may have been found on the trail or site

Before building an outdoor bulletin board, give careful thought to the type of information that you wish to convey. Visit parks and nature centers in your area to find examples of bulletin boards that might meet your needs. Also, check with local career/vocational centers and technical schools to see whether a bulletin board project might be of interest to one of their classes.

Figure 2.51 This beautiful gate at Barnett Shoals Elementary in Georgia welcomes students to the courtyard learning area inside.

Other Interesting Instructional Elements

As I reflected on my school visits, I realized that there were a few site enhancements that

Figure 2.52a–b Simple entrance arbors to a trail or teaching/meeting area establish a sense of uniqueness or special purpose.

didn't fit neatly into the chapter outline, but are too good to miss. I'm hoping that these examples may prime the pump and inspire a unique addition to your school site.

Labyrinths

A labyrinth is usually an arrangement of circular pathways that take a person to the center and then back out again. A labyrinth should not be confused with a maze, which

Figure 2.53 Bulletin boards like this one can generate interest and provide important information at the entrance of an outdoor learning site.

Figure 2.54 This labyrinth is at Forest View Elementary in North Carolina.

frequently has several dead ends and challenges the participant to find a solution.

Although labyrinths have been a part of spiritual practice for centuries, they are appearing more and more frequently on school grounds (see Figure 2.54). By walking a labyrinth, students can reflect, concentrate, and focus. Labyrinths also have a strong connection with history, geometry, and spatial awareness. For many, its greatest appeal is the peaceful respite that it can create for children. A labyrinth also adds a strong element of visual interest to an open area.

Water Features

Water always attracts kids! Many schools take advantage of this powerful attraction by including various types of water elements on the site. Some schools incorporate a whole pond into their site (see Figures 2.55a and b).

Figure 2.55a–b This school in Ohio used a retention basin on the school grounds to create a full-fledged pond. A teaching area was constructed to extend over the water, and tiered seating was installed as another work area and to provide an outdoor performance area with the pond as a backdrop.

Although a pond is a great feature, it just isn't a viable option for many schools. Liability is an often-raised, and very valid, concern. In many communities, the installation of a pond on a school site may also require fencing or other protective enhancements, which can greatly increase cost. A pond is nice, but smaller water features can work very well also. Some schools have created small wetland areas (Figures 2.56 and 2.57). Others have installed small pond-like water features (Figure 2.58). Mini–pond liners available from any garden store make it easy to create a water feature nearly anywhere.

Figure 2.56 Park Forest Elementary in Pennsylvania installed this wetland area right on the school grounds next to the building. Working with the national nonprofit organization Environmental Concern (www.wetland.org), the school received a grant and on-site help as well as staff development concerning educational usage of the wetland. On planting day in spring 2009, every child had an opportunity to place a plant in the newly formed wetland.

Figure 2.57 This tiny wetland model was constructed in a school courtyard in North Carolina.

A water feature is another item that I recommend placing on the "future goals" list rather than the "immediate tasks" agenda. Before even a small plastic pond liner is installed, the parties involved need to consider the following questions:

Figure 2.58 Ford Elementary near Atlanta added this water feature to create an attractive beauty spot at the side of the building.

- How will the feature be used (curriculum enhancement or, mainly, beautification)?
- How will safety and health questions from parents be addressed?
- Who will be responsible for maintaining the feature?
- What legal or insurance requirements must be considered?

Birds: Instant Attention Grabbers

After the teaching/meeting area has been established, my next suggestion is for schools to begin brainstorming ways to attract birds to the site. Birds are wonderful teaching aids that are easy to see and entertaining to watch, and they involve other benefits:

- Birds are very easy to attract to feeders regardless of where you live.
- Feeders can be made very inexpensively by students.
- Birds are around in every season of the year.
- Caring for feeders or birdhouses fosters feelings of stewardship in children.

Students can participate in citizen science projects like Project Feeder Watch through the Cornell Lab of Ornithology (www.birds.cornell.edu/pfw).

The simplest way to get students interested in birds is to place a feeder outside the classroom window. Some shrubs or a nearby tree can provide the shelter and cover that will make the feeder more appealing to birds in the area.

Several schools that I visited have constructed bird blinds on the site. Although these can take a variety of forms, the premise is the same—find a way for children to watch birds without being seen. Figures 2.59 and 2.60 show some options for outdoor bird blinds and describe their origins and uses.

Figure 2.59a–b This bird blind at Forest View Elementary in Durham, North Carolina, is a well-designed structure that functions beautifully both as a bird blind and as a sheltered meeting area that can accommodate a classroom of students. After entering the building, students look out through the open slit that runs the length of the structure. Students make drawings of the birds they have seen and these are mounted on both sides of the building. Several types of bird feeders are located near the viewing area to attract as many types of birds as possible.

I found a great adaptation of the bird blind concept at Brookside Elementary in Worthington, Ohio—an indoor bird blind! Brookside was built during the era when courtyards were very popular. On one glass wall that looks out onto a courtyard, students carefully placed paper with just a few viewing slits left uncovered (see Figure 2.61). Principal Fritz Monroe explains that this bird blind was set up when students wondered why birds were eating more from one feeder in the courtyard than the other. Their hypothesis was that the high

Figure 2.60 This blind is at Park Forest Elementary in State College, Pennsylvania. It is essentially just a wall with openings at varying heights to accommodate students from all grade levels. Since it is not a building, it is far less complex to build than the blind shown in Figure 2.59a and b, but it still serves the same basic function. Notice how the plantings near the blind soften the impact of the structure and provide cover for birds.

Figure 2.61 Two Brookside Elementary students peer out from their indoor bird blind to see how many birds are eating at the feeders in the courtyard.

volume of student traffic visible through the window kept birds away. The bird blind was a way to test the idea. Students made posters explaining why the bird blind was there and kept tallies as to how many birds were eating at the feeders before and after the blind was installed.

It was in Gainesville, Georgia, that I saw the niftiest site enhancement for observing birds truly up close. Teacher Carol Sowers uses a birdhouse with a small camera placed inside at the top (see Figure 2.62a and b). A cable is then run into the building so students can watch the nesting activity inside on a screen. A microphone is part of the camera, so students can hear as well as see the birds. I found information about purchasing these cameras at the following

Figure 2.62a–b This birdhouse has a camera and microphone inside, so students can observe visiting birds without disturbing them.

Web sites: www.birdhousespycam.com and www.gardeningwithkids.org. A Google search of keywords such as "bird house spy cams" will give the latest information about available sources. Most suppliers provide a birdhouse, camera, and cable. Although the equipment may cost around $100, it can be used for many years, and might be a project that could be funded by a parent organization fund-raiser.

Birdhouses are a fun addition to the school grounds. They come in all shapes, colors, and sizes, and sometimes seem more focused on decoration than avian lodging. But that's OK—hopefully any birdhouse will generate interest and help children become a bit more curious about these fascinating animals.

A local nature center can give you excellent advice on the types of birds that might frequent birdhouses on your site, as well as ideas for the style and construction of a suitable dwelling. Some schools have had scout troops set up and maintain bluebird trails or other types of nesting locations on the grounds. If you are serious about attracting nesting birds, it is important to get advice from knowledgeable people. Understanding some basic information can make the difference between houses that are continually empty and active nests. Figures 2.63 through 2.65 show just a few of the variations in birdhouses that are possible.

* * * * * *

I hope you have had a few "aha" moments as you looked through this chapter. I feel confident that some of the enhancements presented here may have sparked your interest and creativity.

Keep in mind that all outdoor classrooms are both unique and dynamic. By unique I mean that what is placed in your outdoor learning area has to be site specific. The list of factors that contributes to the uniqueness of your site is extensive and certainly includes the following:

• Size of the school grounds

Figure 2.63

- Topography and existing natural features
- Space available for outdoor learning enhancements
- Staff interest and level of involvement
- Availability of volunteer help
- Funding possibilities

Your outdoor classroom not only should be tailored to site specific concerns but also should be viewed as a dynamic work in progress. As teachers come and go over the years, the type and frequency of outdoor learning activities will fluctuate also. Topics emphasized in the curriculum change as the years pass, which may result in the site being used for very different types of teaching activities. For example, one Pennsylvania school district recently added a new curriculum strand that focused on wetlands. As a result, a school in the district added a wetland area to its outdoor classroom.

When planning outdoor learning enhancements, it's critical to begin the process by asking two questions:

1. How will the site be used?
2. What specific topics in the curriculum will be enriched through outdoor learning?

If the planning process begins with these two questions, the resulting site enhancements will be useful and well accepted by teachers.

Figure 2.64

Figure 2.65

Spotlight 2
Walking with Georgia

Georgia Gómez-Ibáñez is a soft-spoken lady. She also is an incredibly inspiring, enthusiastic, and energetic lady. Georgia's story has lessons for all of us—not just about outdoor learning, but also about the power of quiet, life-enhancing enthusiasm to change lives.

Georgia teaches at Cambridge Elementary in Cambridge, Wisconsin. When she began her work as a kindergarten classroom aide in 1971, she and the teacher realized quickly that children had an affinity for the outdoors, which resulted in teaching much of the curriculum with an outdoor focus. After participating in an Earth Partnership Institute in 1992, Georgia focused her attention on enriching her schoolyard and planning outdoor activities for all of the K–5 students in the building.

When the elementary school moved to a new site at the edge of town, complete with on-campus woods and a wetland prairie, Georgia arranged her schedule so that she could take all K–5 students outdoors for regular walks that included stewardship and restoration activities. She quickly realized the tremendous impact that resulted from even brief encounters with nature. Just a little walk outside was soothing and calming for children because it moved them away from the noisy and gimmicky world that they were so used to.

Walking Away Problems

Georgia's walking theory got a major test when she was asked to help a fifth-grade boy who was always getting into trouble on the bus ride home. A teacher suggested that Georgia try taking the boy for a twenty-minute walk near the end of the day. So Georgia and the boy walked, sometimes talking, sometimes not—it was up to him. The results were amazing. As a result of that twenty-minute walk, the boy never had problems on the bus again.

News of Georgia's success with the fifth grader spread quickly, and soon teachers referred students to Georgia for regular recess-time walks. She notes that students seem to welcome the opportunity to just be away from the mainstream of noise and distractions for a while.

What makes this story especially powerful is that Georgia officially retired in 2005 but never stopped her walking program. In fact, she is still at the school every day, often putting in eight- to ten-hour days.

A Walk Turns into a Program

This is the cover of a book Georgia created with primary students using their observations on the school grounds.

Bumblebees!
getting that flower stuff,
pollinating,
striped and furry,
slow, then hurry,
flying, fuzzy,
humming, buzzy
Bumblebees!
in the tall, tall prairie.

A Page from "In the Tall, Tall, Prairie."

Georgia now facilitates two kinds of walks: exploring walks and stewardship walks. As the name suggests, an exploring walk involves taking a look at the natural surroundings. These are not just random wanderings, however. Georgia has a lesson plan in mind and modifies what she is doing for the time of year as well as for the curriculum. In early September, for example, she does a "Bug Words Walk" with primary-age children. They look at what the bugs are eating, how they are moving, and where they are living. Georgia writes down the words that children use to describe what they see. They then come back inside and make a book she calls "In the Tall, Tall Prairie," based on the words that were generated outside.

Stewardship walks give students an opportunity to care for the school grounds and their outdoor learning areas. Georgia's school is blessed with an adjoining school forest in which she and her students have developed nature trails over the years. Students on stewardship walks do basic trail maintenance, such as trimming and clearing. Students also develop new trails, carefully transplanting any plants that will be disturbed by the new route. In the fall, a stewardship walk may include gathering seeds from plants in the prairie and spreading them in areas that need enrichment.

The walking program has become somewhat formalized and resembles a "special," much like art, music, or physical education. For example, in grades one through three Georgia works with every child, usually taking one-third of a classroom at a time to keep group sizes manageable on her walks. The program also includes grades four and five, although scheduling is a little more difficult at those grade levels. Georgia walks with her small groups, helping children to observe and record what they see. A current emphasis includes helping students understand phenology (the correlation of climate and periodic biological phenomena, like bird migration). Georgia carefully records daily findings on large wheels that represent the months of the year (see Figure 3.2 in Chapter 3). She also continues to take children for walks as a recess alternative.

But Georgia's day doesn't always end when the bell rings. She has started two after-school environmental education clubs. The focus is often on habitat assessment, which then leads to a discussion of projects that the group could do to improve the habitat.

"Every School Needs a Georgia"

Remember that Georgia is retired! She meets with many students a week, creates lessons, and conducts an after-school program all as a volunteer. I asked Georgia why she chooses to become more involved than ever at the school, rather than sit back and relax in retirement. She answered my question with a beautiful story.

As she was exploring one of her favorite local parks, an old beat-up car drove up, and a rather scruffy looking young man got out. Although she was wary at first, she was amazed to see him take from his car the fanciest camera that she had ever seen. When the young man noticed her he beamed a wide grin and said, "Mrs. G-I, remember me?" It was a former student who had taken many of those walks with Georgia while he was in elementary school—a student, Georgia recalled, who could have headed down a "not-so-good road." He now was a successful freelance photographer doing sophisticated custom photography for university faculty who needed images of specific types of wildlife to include in books and articles. Delighted to see her, he confided, "You, know, I still don't read so good, Mrs. G-I, but if anybody needs a picture of a whatever, I know where to get it!"

How fortunate for this man that he had met Georgia Gómez-Ibáñez early in his school career. Without a doubt, her love of nature, coupled with her belief in the inherent goodness in each child, nurtured him and provided the confidence to develop his special areas of intelligence. Indeed, this story provides a marvelous example of the multiple intelligences concept—although the young man may still not be a great reader, he definitely is very intelligent in other ways. He has an artistic eye with a camera as well as a great awareness of the natural world around him. As Georgia says, "You never know who is getting something really special from the experiences you provide."

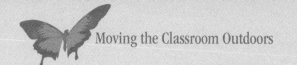

Rachel Carson talked about the need for every child to have an adult who can help to keep the inborn sense of wonder alive (Carson 1956). For Georgia, that adult was her grandmother. Georgia affectionately recalls, "She took me out into the wonderful outdoors and introduced me to a world that has never failed me."

Georgia's mission is to help her students find that world outside that will never fail them. She is convinced that children who spend quality time outdoors develop a special connectedness with nature that provides delight, support, and even comfort. "And," she adds, "then they are more likely to be OK, regardless of what else may be going on in their world."

Each day, Georgia's quiet, life-enhancing enthusiasm continues to help children explore nature and find that sense of wonder that will never fail them. A friend of hers put it very succinctly: "Every school needs a Georgia."

Chapter 3
Outdoor Teaching: Tips and Tricks, Gimmicks and Grabbers

"See the outdoors as a toolbox. Let the natural setting provide examples and manipulatives." That's the philosophy of Sally Massengale, a teacher in Chapel Hill, North Carolina, who is an avid user of the outdoors as an instructional tool. I like the analogy of a toolbox. To be most effective, outdoor instruction needs to be viewed as one of many instructional options that teachers can use to develop and reinforce curricular concepts. Since students learn in different ways and content varies in terms of its applicability in an outdoor setting, outdoor learning is simply one of several instructional options available for developing a lesson.

When talking about outdoor activities, it's useful to remember the distinction between venue and content discussed in Chapter 1. There are times when the outdoors can directly relate to content being taught. After an indoor presentation about geometric shapes, a trek to the schoolyard to find the same shapes in nature can make an abstract concept much more concrete. However, sometimes the outdoors can simply provide an invigorating change of pace and place. Moving the class outdoors occasionally for a discussion or an activity that works equally well either inside or out provides a change of venue that is refreshing and energizing for both student and teacher.

This chapter is both an activity sampler and a sharing of some of the best tips and tricks for outdoor learning that I learned from teachers around the

country. I hope you find useful examples of how teachers are using the outdoors as a tool to teach content. But the chapter goes beyond activities to also focus on very practical methods, approaches, and even simple equipment for facilitating outdoor instruction. The ideas presented here will help you either to enrich your outdoor teaching or to provide the confidence to give this powerful tool a try.

Observation, Signs of Life, and Phenology

Teachers repeatedly mention that a primary goal of outdoor learning is to make children more observant. Improved observation skills transfer outside of the school day also. One teacher shared how a student burst into his classroom and said, "I saw tracks on my way to school today!" Although the child had probably passed tracks dozens of times before, a lesson about tracks in the schoolyard had made this child more alert even when he wasn't in school.

If you live in an area that receives snow, going outside to look for "track stories" after a fresh snowfall is great fun. Wisconsin teacher Matt Tiller takes advantage of the "January thaw" that usually occurs in snowy areas and has students look for the mazes of little tunnels that are uncovered when snow melts in an open field. Matt calls it looking for mouse condominiums. This great sign-of-life activity is based on a description found in Aldo Leopold's *Sand County Almanac*:

> *The mouse is a sober citizen who knows that the grass grows in order that mice may store it as underground haystacks, and that snow falls in order that mice may build subways from stack to stack: supply, demand, and transport all neatly organized. To the mouse, snow means freedom from want and fear. (1986, 4)*

With the low cost of digital cameras, teachers are able to have children create scrapbooks, posters, and phenology wheels with pictures that students have taken (see Figure 3.1). By observing a small area closely over time, students become amazingly adept at detecting even small changes. Excitement erupted at one Pennsylvania school when students saw a tiny patch of grass emerge as the winter snow began to melt. In a world dominated by computer imagery and electronic beeps, how refreshing to have students thrilled to see a few blades of grass emerging from under the snow!

Figure 3.1 This poster from Park Forest Elementary in Pennsylvania displays photos that students of Kristy Stroschein took of their observations outside.

Georgia Gómez-Ibáñez creates a "phenology wheel" with her students (see Figure 3.2). Each year she has the students pick a spot where they will stand and take a picture each month. They arrange the pictures in a circle. She also has students create another wheel that is divided by month. On it, students keep track of what they notice as seasons change. To guide the observations, she has a checklist that provides a general outline of natural changes that can be expected as the seasons progress. The list helps students focus attention on plants, animals, and habitats where they are most likely to see change at a given time of year.

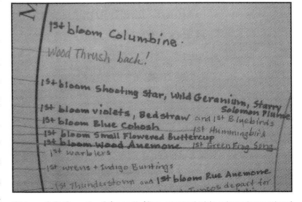

Figure 3.2 Georgia Gómez-Ibáñez created this phenology wheel with her students to record seasonal observations.

Observing Patterns in Longitudinal Data

The ability to identify patterns is critical to most any area of study. Mathematicians, historians, linguists, musicians, artists, and scientists all need to identify patterns in data related to their disciplines. Being able to identify the normal, as well as the abnormal, is useful in all areas of study. The natural world provides a wonderful laboratory for studying patterns:

- At one Ohio school, meter sticks are placed next to milkweed plants. Students then record the growth that occurs every two days (Figure 3.3).
- Bird feeders placed near a classroom window can stimulate data gathering and analysis and can nurture questions such as these:

    How many species visit the feeder?

    Are there peak times of activity at the feeder?

    Does the weather or temperature influence feeding?

A longer-term project at a Wisconsin school requires locating examples of large, medium, and small trees of the same species. The trees are then labeled and the circumference is measured. The plan is to track the growth over several years and analyze the data.

Figure 3.3 Students use this meter stick to measure the growth of milkweed plants every two days.

A Change of Pace and Place

A teacher in Pennsylvania summed up the need for a change of pace and place very well: "Think outside of the school. We work in a box—the classroom."

A teacher in Asheville, North Carolina, describes how he will take a sleepy class outside for a very brief, spontaneous walk. The sluggishness vanishes and students are ready to focus when they return to the classroom.

Working on spelling words can be tedious. Going outside, however, can provide a refreshing change. One Ohio teacher takes her class outside and has kids spell words on the sidewalk (see Figure 3.4). Another teacher used new snowfall to maximum advantage by having students spell words in the snow.

Barnett Shoals Elementary in Georgia certainly has changed the place and scale of teaching basic geology concepts by constructing an impressive geology wall on the school grounds (see Figure 3.5a and b). Students no longer have to be limited to looking at small samples of rocks in egg cartons—they just step outside and see large examples in a natural

Figure 3.4 Taking students outside for typical classroom activities can invigorate them. Practicing spelling words is much more engaging when you use sidewalk chalk!

Figure 3.5a–b Although this geology wall is beautifully constructed and professionally labeled, it certainly would be possible to construct smaller versions and use handout materials to identify the various rocks.

setting. It's a great way for students to see larger examples of local rocks and minerals than can be brought into the classroom. Near the geology wall is a working solar panel to show students that solar energy is more than just a topic in a textbook (see Figure 3.6).

Figure 3.6 Bringing students outside to see this working solar panel takes a discussion of alternative energy resources from abstract concept to concrete example.

Using Books as a Springboard

Florence Milutinovic of Park Forest Elementary in State College, Pennsylvania, has found a wonderful way to incorporate outdoor learning into a unit about prehistoric life. She takes her students outside and reads *If the Dinosaurs Came Back* by Bernard Most to her second-grade class. This whimsical children's book entertains kids by showing dinosaurs in a modern-day setting, catching lost kites and pushing away rain clouds. She then poses the question, "What if dinosaurs came to our schoolyard?" Students then draw pictures of what that might look like and write about what they think might happen. Creativity as well as a sense of scale come out as kids write things like, "They would eat all the leaves" or "They would give children rides."

As students continue to learn more about dinosaurs, Florence poses the question, "Could dinosaurs fit in our schoolyard?" She then cuts yarn to the lengths of various types of dinosaurs—the longest was 180 feet, while the smallest was three feet in length. The students take the yarn outside and judge for themselves where the various dinosaurs might be able to go on the school grounds. As a culminating activity, dinosaur "eggs" are hidden on the schoolyard, and the class troops outside for a new twist on the traditional egg hunt.

The dinosaur-in-the-schoolyard activity is a great example of using the outdoors as a venue for learning. Although Florence could have read the book to students seated in a classroom, the concept of a dinosaur and the scenarios portrayed in the book are enhanced by an outdoor setting. Simply talking indoors about the size of dinosaurs just doesn't make the same dramatic impression that is created when twenty-five kids hold 180 feet of yarn and try to imagine the body that occupied such a large space.

Park Forest teachers also suggest two books by Lois Ehlert as great springboards for outdoor activity and discussion. One is *Leaf Man* (2005), a delightful picture book that tells a story with leaf collages that take the form of different shapes and animals. The book can inspire wonderful art projects using fall leaves, and most certainly makes children more aware of the variety, beauty, and complexity of the autumn landscape. What a great precursor to a walk!

Planting a Rainbow is another Ehlert (1988) book designed for primary-level children. The book is a perfect way to build excitement for planting on the school grounds. It begins in the fall and introduces children to several types of familiar bulbs that can be planted on most school sites. Beautiful pictures then show the springtime flowers that emerge from the bulbs. The book progresses to familiar annual flowers that can be planted as the weather warms. I love the last third of the book, which shows the spectacular colors found in common flowers around the schoolyard and in home gardens. The color section would be a perfect segue into an outdoor color-matching activity. I like to use paint chip samples (usually readily available from paint or home improvement stores if you explain that you are a teacher) and have children try to match the paint sample with something outdoors.

At the primary grades, there are hundreds of picture books that can create enthusiasm for outdoor exploration. Like the books described above, many books written for very young readers immediately and almost instinctively lead to outdoor activities.

Chapter books for older readers often don't generate outdoor activity ideas as obviously as *Planting a Rainbow*, but the activities of characters, the theme, or the setting of a book frequently can inspire creative use of the outdoors. Teachers have created simulated archaeological digs on the school grounds, planted gardens with plants mentioned in literature, and even staged reenactments of Civil War battles to complement books read in class.

The National Outdoor Book Awards (NOBA) Web site is good place to begin looking for books with an outdoor theme. The National Outdoor Book Awards Foundation, along with the Association of Outdoor Recreation and Education and Idaho State University, sponsors the award for this nonprofit educational program. The program was founded in 1997 and includes a children's books category. On their Web site (www.noba-web.org), you can look at lists of book winners for every year since the program began. Interestingly, the current prevalence of social issues and commentary topics in young adult literature has made the traditional outdoor-themed book harder to find.

Cross-Grade Activities

The idea of pairing older students with younger ones has been around for a long time. It's very common to see "buddies" from the intermediate grades working with primary students on a variety of activities, including reading, composition, and art projects. Traditionally, however, much of the "buddy"

work has taken place within the confines of the school building. The benefits of cross-grade learning experiences are just as great, however, when learning moves outdoors.

In Verona, Wisconsin, cross-grade learning experiences in the outdoors are thriving. Matt Tiller, science teacher at Verona Area High School, and Liz Penner, teacher of grades one and two at Glacier Edge Elementary, are encouraging and coordinating efforts to pair high school students with elementary kids. The results have been inspiring.

To have high school students share their enthusiasm for the outdoors has a strong impact on young children. Younger students naturally look up to older students and can be easily influenced by their likes, dislikes, and interests. But the impact works in reverse also. When a high schooler is placed in the role of mentor to a young child, there is a subtle pressure for the older student to look even more closely at nature to generate meaningful questions and responses. It's the old story—when you help someone learn about or explore something new, you usually gain a greater understanding and appreciation also.

Because Matt and Liz have been working with cross-grade learning for a few years now, they have picked up some helpful tips for combining grade levels in the outdoors. Although their experience has been with a high school/ elementary mix, many of these ideas would work well with a pairing of upper elementary or middle school with elementary children. A few of their ideas, and ideas from other teachers, are described in the following sections.

Preparing Older Students for Working with Younger Students

Effective cross-grade learning requires more than just pairing students and walking outside. Matt takes the time to prepare his high school students with the basics of inquiry teaching. First, of course, the high school students need to be comfortable with the science content that will be encountered outdoors. But far more important, Matt teaches them how to engage little kids with the nature they are seeing. The key, he says, is to emphasize the need for "asking questions and probing and probing and probing." For example, when primary students notice a hole in a tree and ask why it's there, the older student should not just say, "It's probably a woodpecker's nest." Instead, the high schooler is encouraged to expand inquiry by asking, "What do you think?" Other questions then follow and build on the responses of the younger children:

- What could have made that hole? What kind of animal?
- What kinds of animals live around here?
- Would the animal be in there to live, or is the animal after food?
- If it's after food, what kind of food might the animal be looking for?

It's tough to get older students to refrain from immediately giving an answer; to naturally respond with probing questions takes a bit of practice. Of course, even as experienced teachers, we often are tempted to go immediately to the answer rather than encourage students to reflect and explore.

Pairing Students

When Matt and Liz first began to organize cross-grade learning experiences, they paired one high school student with one elementary student. After many attempts and much reflection, they now recommend forming groups of two or three high school students with two or three elementary children. These slightly larger groups seem to generate a higher level of comfort for both the high school kids and their elementary counterparts.

Buddy Writing Day

Twelfth-grade creative writing students are paired with first graders for a unique shared composition experience called "Buddy Writing Day" (see Figure 3.7). This late-spring activity was developed by teachers Sue Wainwright, Erin Martin, and Holly Dionne. The primary objective is to use sensory detail to describe a selected focal point on the school site through a poem or paragraph.

High school students get to know their "little buddies" and encourage dialogue by initially asking some general questions and telling a little about themselves:

- What is your name? My name is . . .
- What do you like to do when you aren't in school? My hobbies are . . .
- What kinds of things do you like to write? I like to write . . .

Figure 3.7 High school and elementary students gather for Buddy Writing Day in Verona, Wisconsin.

- What is your favorite part of school? My favorite part is . . .
- What will you do for fun this summer? I will . . .

The questions are an important part of the process and are planned in advance. This informal chat puts both high school and elementary students at ease and establishes a positive rapport and beginning point for sharing observations in nature. The high school students have preselected interesting outdoor spots to use as focal points. Sites are chosen because they feature something that is unique or fosters curiosity. Rotting logs, nests of all types, unusual plants and flowers, spider webs, and so on are frequently used as focal points.

Figure 3.8 A Big Buddy records the observations of her Little Buddy.

After arriving at the special spots, the high school students serve as recorders as first graders offer their observations orally (see Figure 3.8). A sheet has been prepared that has the questions and space to record responses of both the big and little buddies:

What details did you notice?
Little Buddy:
Big Buddy:

Some of the other questions include the following:

Can you see any patterns or interesting things?
What colors do you see?
Do these colors remind you of anything else from another place?
What shapes do you see?
Do these shapes remind you of something from another place?
If you could touch this without hurting it or you, how do you think it would feel?
Do you notice any sounds around us, or is the object we're describing making any sound? How would you describe these sounds?
Do these sounds remind you of something you have heard before?
If this object could talk, what do you think it would say to us?

When each question has been answered by both the younger and the older students, the older student reads the draft to the younger one. The pair discusses any need for changes or revisions to the responses. The final product can then be turned into a poem or a descriptive paragraph. The older students then thank their little buddies and take their drafts back to the classroom for refining. Great care is used not to significantly alter the language used by the first graders.

At a later time, the high school students share their work with the elementary students. Sometimes the sharing is done during the next visit to the school forest at the high school. At other times, the high school students go directly to the elementary to share the poems. Recently, Matt started to use Skype to video-conference with his class and the elementary students. The Skype session is done using SMART Boards in both classrooms so all students can easily see one another. What a great use of technology to maintain a connection and to culminate an activity!

The activity is simple yet very powerful. Although Verona pairs high school seniors with first graders, this same type of activity could work well at a variety of grade levels. It's especially easy to do if both grade levels are in the same building. Eighth graders can work well with fifth graders in a middle school, or fifth graders can enjoy working with first graders.

Soil Sampling

The idea of first and second graders doing soil profiles may seem a bit unusual. In Verona, however, soil profiles decorate the walls of elementary classrooms (see Figure 3.9a–c). Matt Tiller uses a soil auger to bring up samples at 1 foot increments going down to 5 feet at various locations on the school site: wetland, wood-

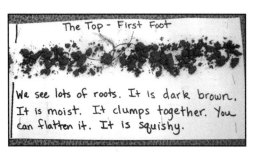

Figure 3.9a–c Soil samples from different depths are analyzed by high school students and their elementary buddies.

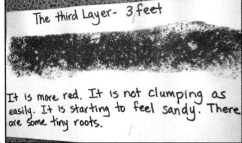

Figure 3.10 High school teacher Matt Tiller demonstrates soil sampling to elementary students.

land, and prairie (see Figure 3.10). His high school students then help the younger students they work with bag and label the soils and encourage them to note differences and describe the soils. The bags are then taken back to the elementary school for further description. Students use the bagged soil to make a soil profile.

Students also explore how water moves through soil. They pour water into jars to create filters containing gravel, sand, or clay. Some students noticed that the water moved more quickly in some jars than in others. That concept was then applied to the soil samples they had just collected. They asked, How might water flow differently through the types of soils that we have on our profiles?

Matt and his students provided examples of plants with varying root structures that had been collected near the areas where the soil samples were taken (wetland, woodland, and prairie). Elementary students were asked how the root structures might vary in different types of soils to help plants get needed water and nutrients.

Although Verona has a range of habitats on the school site, the soil sampling project easily can be done in environments that are less varied. Most school grounds have wet areas, grassy areas, garden or flower beds, and so on, which can provide the diversity needed for this type of study.

Wisconsin Fast Plants

To be honest, I had never heard of Fast Plants until I visited Wisconsin. According to the Fast Plants Web site, "Fast Plants® are a type of crucifer (a large group of plants that includes mustard, radish, cabbage, and more) that have been bred and selected to have a uniform, short flowering time (14 days) and grow well in a small indoor space, with little soil, under artificial lights"

(Wisconsin Fast Plants 2010). Since leaves appear very quickly and flowers bloom in fourteen to seventeen days, these plants provide wonderful opportunities for classroom research projects.

Matt Tiller's high school students use the plants to study pollination and plant genetics. Liz Penner's elementary students grow the plants also, but they focus on the life cycle of insects. Cabbage white butterfly larvae feed on the Fast Plants and provide an opportunity to study the metamorphosis of the caterpillar to the butterfly. In the spring, Matt's students join with Liz's students and both age groups share what they have learned by using the Fast Plants. It's a great opportunity to show that research transcends grade levels and can be engaging at any age.

With students at grades four and five, a mixture of Fast Plant seeds are planted. The objective is for students to look carefully at the plants that emerge and identify differences and relationships among the plants. For example, plants with purple stems are usually short, while plants with light green leaves are tall. By growing the plants, collecting data, and then looking for relationships, students engage in real scientific activity. In the spring, the skill of looking for relationships in nature is reinforced when students make a trip to the forest at the high school and look for relationships at the outdoor site.

Nature Clubs

As I visited schools that emphasize outdoor learning, I was impressed with the number that provide an after-school club or program to extend learning opportunities for interested students. Sometimes these clubs are very informal, with most of the activity being student directed—just a chance to poke around in nature. Others are more formal, with distinct themes for each year or even each month.

Nature clubs usually focus on one or more of these dimensions of outdoor experience:

Environmental responsibility. Club members work on projects that will improve the school or community environment. An after-school nature club may take on projects like a recycling campaign or an energy usage awareness program. Frequently, it is the nature club that becomes the environmental conscience of a building.

Stewardship and maintenance. School site enhancements always require periodic maintenance. A trail or pathway, for example, will soon become overgrown if there is not annual trimming. Bird feeders must be filled, gardens need occasional weeding, and something is always in need of repair. These routine, but essential, tasks need to be done if an outdoor learning area is to stay viable and appealing. Since it's not realistic to expect school maintenance employees to take on the increased workload of maintaining an outdoor learning site, nature clubs can provide welcome and needed help. More important, students develop a sense of pride and ownership when they take an active role in maintaining an area. Most schoolyard developers concur that a feeling of ownership on the part of students readily translates into reduced problems with vandalism on outdoor learning sites.

Extension and enrichment experiences. Since nature clubs usually have rather small membership numbers, it's easy to arrange for special outings to nature centers or local parks. Frequently, parents form car pools to drive children to locations, thereby saving the cost of bus transportation.

Specialized enrichment experiences usually are planned right on the school site. One after-school nature club has taken on the challenge of developing new trails every year in a wooded area that adjoins the school grounds. When the new trail is cleared, an existing trail is closed and as many plants as possible are transplanted to fill in the previous trail location. Students not only have the challenge of creating a new trail, but they also get some up-close contact with the plants that they may never have taken the time to notice.

Nature clubs provide opportunities for kids to explore further and to develop relationships with adults who sincerely appreciate the outdoors. One Pennsylvania teacher said that a nature club changed how children used recess time. Many kids are now voluntarily spending time looking for unusual plants, insects, animal signs, and fossils on the playground.

Garden Tips

When most schools describe their schoolyard learning efforts, gardens or specialized plantings usually are mentioned as important components of a program. Even schools in northern climates frequently provide planting opportunities for students. Chapter 2 gives several specific examples of garden enhancements and structural elements. The following sections provide some tips that may be helpful as you consider planting on your site.

Rain Barrels

If you plan to have a garden area or special plantings on your site, watering can pose a problem. Rain barrels collect the water either from downspouts or as freestanding containers, although downspouts fill barrels faster. Barrels have a spigot at the bottom and can hold enough water to take care of a small garden area. Rain barrels can be purchased through home improvement stores or from Internet sites. Often schools make their own from donated materials (see Figure 3.11).

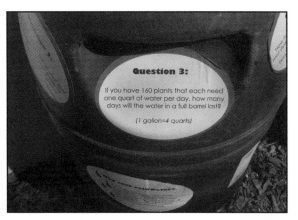

Question 3:

If you have 160 plants that each need one quart of water per day, how many days will the water in a full barrel last?

(1 gallon=4 quarts)

Figure 3.11 The Evergreen Community Charter School in Asheville, North Carolina, uses its rain barrel as a billboard for environmental learning and consciousness.

Tips from Granny

Roberta Paolo, founder of Granny's Garden School in Ohio, has many practical ideas for starting and maintaining a garden program:

- Begin in front of the school by planting flowers. Colorful blooms get people's attention and provide something to give away.
- Roberta gives away thousands of flowers each year. Her Bouquets on Wheels program for senior citizens is described in Spotlight 5 on page 172. In addition, her school gardens provide perennials for Habitat for Humanity houses. What a wonderful way to provide meaningful service projects while building positive public relations.
- Although many garden plants will not bloom or be edible until after school is out for the summer, Roberta tries to have students plant something that can be harvested before the school year ends. Many greens are fast growing and can provide a salad before the year ends. For other flowers and crops, the emphasis is on planting forward for the next class.
- Planting different colors of the same vegetable can encourage students to sample a food that they may have already decided they don't like. Radishes, for example, come in a variety of colors, including red, pink, white, yellow,

and purple. Roberta tries to include several varieties of radishes in the same planting bed. Instead of saying, "Let's taste a radish," she turns the statement into a question: "Do you think the purple radish will taste hotter than the white one?" Amazingly, kids who wouldn't think of eating a vegetable are intrigued enough by the question to give it a try!

- Get good shovels. Spending a little extra on good-quality shovels is worth it to avoid breakage.
- Roberta uses e-mail very effectively. She has an e-mail list of parents who have an interest in the gardens. Whenever there is a need for plants or flowerpots or whatever, she just puts the need in an e-mail. Usually, the response is more than adequate to meet the need. Parents are often very eager to help if the item is clearly specified. Simply asking for "help" brings much less response than, for example, asking for empty kitty litter containers, which Roberta feels work better than commercial buckets because they don't stick together (see Figure 3.12).

Figure 3.12 Parents respond in spades when asked for specific items to support a school garden. This school now has plenty of empty kitty litter containers to use as water and plant buckets in their garden!

- Looking for a protective cover for young plants, or a support for growing flowers? Roberta uses empty planters that had been lined with moss in a previous season (see Figure 3.13).
- Roberta has started the unique tradition of planting sunflower seeds on Earth Day. Children plant nearly twenty-five different varieties on the school grounds. The result in late July is spectacular!
- Granny tries to have children take home a brief note that tells parents, "This is what we did in the garden today." It's so important to incorporate information about outdoor teaching in the newsletters or update sheets that

Figure 3.13 Empty wire baskets serve as perfect plant supports.

most teachers send home to parent periodically. Encourage administrators to include brief descriptions and pictures of outdoor learning activities in school newsletters and on school Web sites.

A unique theme

Themed gardens are always popular. One Georgia school has a "dye garden." All of the plants in the garden have been used historically to dye cloth. Students have the opportunity to card wool and then dye cloth. I was told that the teacher who came up with the idea even had the last name of Dye! I really like this theme since it not only involves sowing seeds and weeding but also provides a great opportunity to touch on the historical and economic significance of plants.

Weeding

Keeping up with weeding and other garden chores is always a challenge. A North Carolina teacher uses outdoor work as an "anchor activity" before class starts or when children finish an activity early. His classroom has an exterior door, and the garden plot is located immediately outside in full view of classroom windows. Kids love the opportunity to go outside briefly when work is completed—evidence of the power of a change of pace and place.

Birds as Motivators

Birds provide dynamic teaching opportunities. They can be readily attracted to a school site, they are easy to spot, and they instantly engage student interest.

Some great tips for attracting birds and using them in instructional activities are provided in the following sections. The information is adapted from the Wild School Site Project developed by the Ohio Department of Natural Resources (ODNR) Division of Wildlife. Adapted excerpts are from their award-winning book *Twenty/Twenty: Projects and Activities for Wild School Sites*, written and compiled by Paul Schiff (1996) and presented here with permission.

Perch and Plant

The simple addition of a perching wire to a school site provides a rich source of data to analyze as well as an opportunity to understand the important role of birds in seed dispersal. Old fencerows are often overtaken by trees, shrubs, and vines. But how did they get there? This simple project shows how a fencerow develops.

A wire is stretched between two posts over a strip of tilled ground as a perching place for birds. As birds begin perching on the wire, their droppings will be planting many different types of seeds. As seeds germinate and plants grow, students learn about seed dispersal and the types of food that birds eat.

All vegetation should be cleared from a strip of ground about 3 feet wide and 10 feet long. If practical, remove any sod and work the area with a roto-tiller.

The simplest system would be to erect a salvaged fence post at each end and stretch a clothesline between the posts. A more elaborate, semipermanent system could be developed with channel posts, eyebolts, turnbuckles, and heavy-gauge wire. Salvaged black locust fence posts or purchased, treated 4-by-4-inch posts can be substitutes for iron channel posts. The larger diameter wooden fence posts double as support for the wire and perching platforms for bird species that prefer a post to the wire.

If a single wire or rope is used, it should be 4 to 5 feet above the ground. Two wires or ropes may be used to provide additional perching options.

It won't take long for plants to begin growing under the wire. By keeping track of what birds are observed and what types of plants are growing, students can discover what types of foods the birds prefer and what seed are distributed in the birds' droppings. Many of the plants, as they mature, will begin to provide food and cover for visiting birds and other animals.

Caution: Use great care in deciding where to set up your perch-and-plant area. It's important that the wires not be in an area where people frequently play or pass by. The wire is at a height that could be dangerous to people who are not watching where they are going, especially at night. Some schools place the perch and plant near a low wall or other obstacle that blocks walking or running. Fencing or plantings placed in front of the area also can reduce the risk of someone running into the wire.

For the Birds

Birdhouses provide an inexpensive way to attract wildlife to a school site. Instructions for building birdhouses abound on the Internet. Be sure, though, to investigate what types of birds are most common in your area and check whether special types of houses are required to attract these species. For example, purple martins are attracted to white birdhouses, while many other birds are not. Although wood is the most commonly used birdhouse material, natural items, including sections of hollow logs and dried gourds, can be used also.

Here are some tips for constructing birdhouses from the ODNR:

- Don't use aromatic or chemically treated lumber. The fumes can be harmful to young birds.
- Drill ventilation and drain holes.
- Paint houses with natural colors, such as tan or dull green (except for purple martin houses). Don't paint the inside of the box.
- Locate houses near natural nesting habitat and away from frequent human interference.
- Don't put too many houses in a small area. Many birds are territorial and will not nest close to other birds' nests.
- Clean houses by removing old nesting materials each winter.

The Feeding Station

A single bird feeder will attract a few diners, but a feeding station, with multiple types of feeders, will attract a wide range of visitors and make observation even more interesting for students.

Birds have definite preferences for the kinds of food they like and how they like to eat. Some birds prefer grain and seeds, some fruit, and others are attracted to animal fat (suet). Different birds prefer to feed at different heights, from grain scattered directly on the ground to platforms or feeders elevated on posts or in trees. As you increase the variety of feeders, the variety of species visiting the station will increase also.

A critical point in planning a feeding station is to ensure that there is protective cover nearby. Shelter provided by brush piles, evergreen trees, shrubs, and bushes serve as a staging area as birds wait in line to visit the feeder. Dense cover also provides protection from weather and predators.

Figure 3.14 This feeding station provides several types of feeders at different levels to invite a variety of bird species to dine.

A variety of feeders at various elevations should be included (see Figure 3.14). Feeders designed to dispense a single type of food, such as tube thistle feeders and basket or cage suet feeders, are effective. Simple platforms either raised on a post or near the ground provide easy access. However, the grain must be replaced when it becomes wet or snow covered. Platform feeders with roofs help to keep food dry and available. Grain simply scattered on the ground near cover provides for many species. Dispenser-type hopper feeders have the advantage of storing food to be dispensed as needed, requiring less maintenance.

The more sheltered your feeding station location, the better. Strong winds and open spaces will discourage birds from visiting. Be sure to include water in simple homemade or purchased birdbaths at your feeding station.

Place a feeding station where birds can be easily observed. Bird feeding is intended as a "people" project as much as a wildlife management project. The real joy of bird feeding comes from watching, not just feeding. If possible, locate feeding stations near classroom or cafeteria windows, or in courtyard areas that are visible from several angles.

The ODNR emphasizes that while feeding birds and other wildlife is rewarding and educational, the greatest long-term benefit for students and wildlife would be to incorporate the planting of food-producing plants (shrubs, trees, grain) along with providing feeders.

Moving from Passive "Watching" to Active Exploration

Whether you have a feeding station or just a single feeder, there are activities that can challenge student thinking. The ODNR describes three great activities for observing bird behavior by varying the type of food and how it is presented and assessing the impact of a distraction.

Bird Feed Preference

In order to quantify which food offering is actually preferred by certain birds, a few simple guidelines should be followed: (1) food should be provided in similar amounts; (2) different seeds should be offered in the same manner; and (3) the birds should be counted in the same way each time.

Put equal amounts of three or four different grains (for example, corn, sunflower, and wheat) in similar containers. Small, clay drip trays for potted plants work well. Arrange the trays on a platform where birds have been feeding, or simply place them on the ground. Birds can be observed as they select their preferred food from among those offered. Another option is to remeasure the food after a period of time and see which type was eaten most. Of course, mice or squirrels could upset the experiment!

Color Preference

This is a very simple, yet tremendously engaging, activity. Many common birds, such as blue jays, English sparrows, and starlings, relish table scraps. In this activity, cooked macaroni is offered as food.

Add food coloring to cooked macaroni and offer birds their choice of blue, red, green, or uncolored food. Have students generate predictions about how the birds will react to the colored food. After several days, have students compare their predictions with the actual observations.

Interference

Make or purchase cutouts or models of a snake, owl, or other bird. Place the artificial visitor near the food supply. How do your students think the birds that normally visit the feeding station will react? Using string and screw eyes, the artificial visitors can even be made to move when birds approach.

Special thanks again to the Ohio Department of Natural Resources, Division of Wildlife, and Paul Schiff (1996) for granting permission to reprint much of the material in the preceding section on birds.

Portable Lessons and Equipment

The schoolyard may have several great enhancements, such as a convenient teaching/meeting area, unmowed patches, and specialized plantings, but teachers may still not regularly use the site for instruction. Often, the problem is time. It takes time to gather the necessary materials to teach an outdoor lesson—extra minutes that many teachers just don't have. However, some

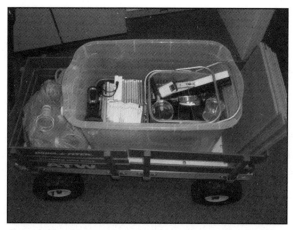

Figure 3.15 Little red wagons are a handy way to store and transport supplies.

Figure 3.16 According to Karan Wood, "Each field study kit teaches one curriculum standard at one grade level and consists of a clear plastic backpack filled with laminated directions for a hands-on student investigation, all necessary supplies for a class of thirty-two, and questions for debriefing the lesson" (Wood 2006, 37).

schools have developed tools that help with this issue.

Park Forest Elementary in State College, Pennsylvania, provides teachers with access to a mini-fleet of little red wagons that are loaded with the types of materials that are frequently needed for an outdoor lesson. The wagons carry magnifiers, lapboards, sampling containers, field guides, measuring tapes, and carrying containers (see Figure 3.15). The wagons are conveniently stored in a workroom near the front door of the school.

Probably the most innovative approach that I have seen to provide teachers with ready access to materials and activities for outdoor teaching was found in Acworth, Georgia. My host was Karan Wood, a volunteer who has worked with faculty, staff, and other volunteers at Frey Elementary School. The school has a tremendous array of outdoor learning enhancements, but what truly impressed me the most were the field study kits that lined the walls of teacher workrooms (see Figure 3.16).

Teachers identified standards that could be effectively enhanced through outdoor instruction and suggested activities that could be placed in the backpacks. The entire project took three years, but encompassed the entire science curriculum in grades K–5. Since the outdoors is highly interdisciplinary, teachers also created backpacks for social studies, math, and language arts.

Although a project of this magnitude would not be feasible everywhere, the idea of selecting a few content standards and then assembling all materials needed in a highly portable container or tote bag can work on any scale. Parent volunteers can be a tremendous help in assembling the needed materials and can oversee the replacement of consumable materials in the kits.

Natural Toys

Bringing natural materials inside to use as playthings provides a nice change from the usual menu of plastic, beeping toys. Sections of tree limbs work just fine for stacking or building (see Figure 3.17).

Figure 3.17 This basket of natural items can amuse young children just as effectively as a brand-name collection of plastic manipulatives.

Bringing in the Outdoors

Interest in the outdoors can frequently be effectively nurtured indoors. Sally Massengale is an educator at Glenwood Elementary in Chapel Hill, North Carolina. Although Sally shared many wonderful outdoor teaching activities with me, I was especially impressed with how hard she worked to build an interest in exploration of the school grounds by creatively displaying outdoor discoveries indoors.

Sally has a simple yet highly interactive way to remind children that there is a rich natural environment that exists just beyond the schoolhouse door (see Figure 3.18). To encourage children to observe their surroundings more carefully, Sally has put up a simple diagram of the school grounds right outside the cafeteria door, probably one of the busiest stretches of hallway in the building. As students find interesting natural specimens of plants or animals, Sally helps them sketch what they saw on an index card and identify what it was. The card is then placed beside the diagram of the school grounds, with a piece of yarn linking the natural item to its location on the diagram. The result is a frequently changing update of what has been discovered on the site. The location of the diagram in a busy area of the building

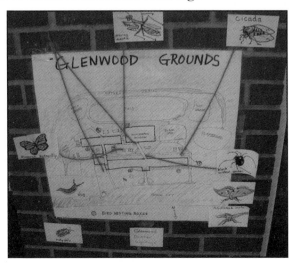

Figure 3.18 This diagram of the grounds of Glenwood Elementary documents the nature observations of students.

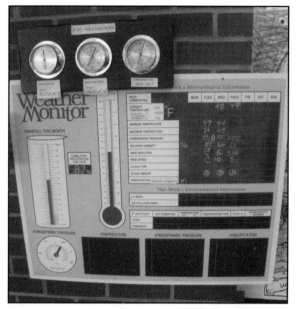

Figure 3.19 Although many teachers track weather data within a classroom, Sally has made this a very public display of environmental information that everyone in the building can see. It sends a powerful message that emphasizes what is happening right around the building.

ensures that that many students will pause and take a look.

In this same area outside of the cafeteria, Sally has set up a simple weather monitoring display (see Figure 3.19). Kids keep track of simple data, like humidity, rainfall, temperature, cloud cover, and so on.

Weather can provide a tremendous amount of data. The cost of weather monitoring equipment has dropped to a point where schools can afford to set up small weather stations linked to classroom computers. Some schools have a weather station on the school roof connected to a PC in a science classroom. The weather station collects data about wind speed and direction, temperature and relative humidity, rainfall, light intensity, barometric pressure, and indoor temperature. This rich accumulation of longitudinal data can provide abundant fodder for all types of analyses and comparisons. The weather observations can even be displayed in real time on a school Web page.

Murals/Artwork

Public art in school hallways can do much to create both awareness and curiosity about the outdoors. Park Forest Elementary in State College, Pennsylvania, uses three-dimensional murals that are created by placing individual pieces of student work into the creation. Soon after the building opened, one stairwell was designated as the site for a tree whose branches hold ceramic leaves and tiles created by students in the building (see Figure 3.20a and b).

The stairwell tree was so successful that another mural was designed using the same concept of integrating individual student artwork (see Figure 3.21a–b). This second mural covers over 10 feet of wall space and, like the first mural, engaged more than forty students from grades three, four, and five to create elements to include in the composition. Public art on this scale inside the building sends a constant message that nature is an important theme at Park Forest.

Figure 3.20a–b This gorgeous stairway art was coordinated by art teacher Melanie Fink and muralist Terri Johnson, whose services were provided through the local arts in education organization, GALAXY, and the Park Forest Elementary Parent Teacher Organization. Individual student work is incorporated into the tree.

Figure 3.21a–b The three-dimensional effect of this mural immediately draws attention, and students proudly point to their personal contributions to the project.

Children's artwork can do so much to brighten up drab places, including fences (see Figure 3.22 and 3.23). Outdoor weaving frames are also becoming increasingly popular on school sites. The idea is very simple. Just set up a frame with strings to form the warp. Students then can weave strips of material, vines, leaves, small branches—whatever they find interesting—into the design (see Figure 3.24).

At Brookside Elementary School in Columbus, Ohio, the school is using the outdoors as a springboard for teaching in a variety of content areas. Decorating one of the hallways at Brookside is some unique student artwork

Figure 3.22 A chain-link fence at Ford Elementary in Acworth, Georgia, has been transformed into a real focal point by placing kids' artwork on it. Notice how this institutional-looking fence almost disappears when the colorful artwork is displayed.

Figure 3.23 A school in the harbor town of Seldovia, Alaska, very appropriately uses fish motifs to liven up a fence.

that uses nature in a social studies lesson about prehistoric civilizations (see Figure 3.25). Sixth-grade students went outside and found small sticks that were sturdy enough to work as brush handles. They then took small bunches of pine needles and fastened them to the sticks with string. To create ambience, teachers had the students take their natural brushes into the gym and turn out the lights. By the glow of flashlights (much safer than candles!) students used paint and the pine brushes to create "cave art" on large sheets of brown paper.

Figure 3.25 Students in Worthington, Ohio, created their own interpretation of cave art using brushes made from natural materials found on the school grounds.

* * * * * *

Think of the outdoors as an instructional toolbox. In any climate, during any season, and in all content areas, nature provides multiple venues and options for enhancing, enriching, and adding a much-needed change of pace and place to the instructional routine. Like a toolbox, the outdoors is readily accessible—just open the classroom door and step outside!

Figure 3.24 This outdoor weaving frame at Ford Elementary in Acworth, Georgia, contains colorful strips of cloth that students have selected. Often, weaving frames also incorporate leaves, sticks, and other natural elements.

Spotlight 3
Professional Development, Park Forest Style

When you walk into the main office of Park Forest Elementary in State College, Pennsylvania, you can't miss the unusual reception counter. It's made of bricks—old bricks from the previous Park Forest School that was located on the same site.

The demolition of the old school was a challenge to principal Donnan Stoicovy. She had long been an advocate for outdoor learning and encouraged the use of the school site for instruction. However, the construction of a new school provided the impetus to rethink how best to encourage outdoor teaching and learning at Park Forest.

Donnan Stoicovy, principal of Park Forest Elementary, and Rebecca West Burns, doctoral candidate and professional development associate

State College and Park Forest

The State College Area School District has 7,100 students in ten elementary schools (K–5), two middle schools, and one high school. Park Forest is the largest elementary school in the district, with 460 students, and "encompasses the widest socio-economic range, the greatest special education cohort, and the top third in race and ethnic diversity for the District's population" (Burns and Stoicovy 2007, 2).

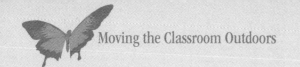

State College, Pennsylvania, is the home of Penn State University (PSU). Park Forest is one of the buildings that participates with PSU in a district-wide Professional Development School (PDS) model that incorporates the district's entire elementary program. The PDS model creates a powerful partnership between the school district and the university. The university contributes expertise concerning best professional practice, and teachers provide input based on daily classroom interaction. The result is a rich blending of both theory and practice.

Park Forest has the unique opportunity to host PSU undergraduate student teaching interns for an entire school year. The novice teachers gain tremendous experience from the opportunity to work for an extended time with practicing professionals, and the faculty benefits from both the energizing influence of enthusiastic future teachers as well as the professional support provided through the PSU College of Education.

The Professional Development Plan

Although Donnan has always been a strong advocate for staff development, her views concerning the nature and delivery of professional growth opportunities have changed over the years. In the past, teachers were exposed to a variety of workshop experiences, including training in the Project WILD and Project Learning Tree materials. Although these whole-faculty staff development experiences were helpful, she felt that there was a need for more individualized and theme-focused professional growth. The one-size-fits-all model of staff development wasn't generating much interest in outdoor learning.

Working with Penn State doctoral student and professional development associate Rebecca Burns, Donnan began the development of a long-range professional development plan for her building. Both Donnan and Rebecca view the schoolyard as an untapped resource often only used for recess and fire drills. However, they see that with a little creative thought and ambition, the schoolyard can evolve as an integrated context for learning.

As the new Park Forest school was being completed, Donnan and a team of teachers attended a course sponsored by the Professional Development School that culminated in the team creating the Schoolyard Project. The purpose of the project was to engage the rest of the staff in exploring ways to use the newly configured schoolyard. The team focused on the central theme of exploring the phenology of the school site. To introduce the theme in the school, Donnan used the book *Window* (1991) by Jeannie Baker as her motivator. *Window* is a marvelous wordless picture book that shows a window frame and the view outside the window. Each of the thirteen double-page images in this beautiful book shows how the scene outside the window changes over time. After sharing the book with all of her students, Donnan explained that they would be exploring changes on the Park Forest school site. Four outdoor areas were selected by teachers and were visited by classrooms each month. Observations were made and recorded in journals. A schoolwide journal for each site was then compiled.

In the fall of 2007, teachers were given an extensive survey to assess their acceptance of the Schoolyard Project as well as to see what types of support might be needed in order to use the outdoors more frequently. The results showed clearly that teachers were very comfortable working with students in the outdoors and that outdoor learning was viewed as both appropriate and desirable. Although the general consensus was that it was good for children to be outside, there often was little being done beyond the once-per-month phenology observations. It became clear that it was necessary to help teachers see how the outdoors could relate directly to the curriculum. The need for help with planning outdoor lessons clearly surfaced from the survey.

The questionnaire also asked teachers to rank the types of professional development that they preferred. Interestingly, "Discuss information with my colleagues" came out with the highest ranking, followed closely by "Have an expert do hands-on experiences." That result led to a pilot study with volunteer teachers the following year.

Donnan acknowledged the importance of collegial discussion by having teachers organize themselves into learning teams. The three teams that emerged were free to set their own agendas and sharpen their own focus using the general theme of schoolyard usage. The expectation was that teams meet monthly, set an agenda, record minutes, share ideas, engage in project work, and reflect on research. Often the teams would use an article or book selected by the group as a discussion starter. Although the highly open structure was a little unsettling to some at first, the results have been meaningful as groups feel empowered to shape their exploration of a topic according to their own needs.

Each of the three groups has developed its own focus regarding the use of the outdoors. One team has concentrated on ways to integrate the outdoors into writing activities, with a major goal being to help students learn how to make science writing authentic. Another team chose to explore ways to relate literature to the schoolyard, primarily by finding read-aloud books that could be used effectively in an outdoor setting. The third group developed more of an art-in-nature focus, with the goal of helping children to see that there were options to traditional writing for expressing what they experienced outdoors.

Gratifying Results

The three teams have evolved as powerful professional growth experiences. As one teacher noted, the teams help to solidify a vision and purpose for going outside. Outdoor activities become a part of a unified plan rather than isolated "once and done" experiences.

Although not all teachers in the building are involved in the pilot efforts, there has been a definite ripple effect. As one teacher points out, "There are enough of us that the enthusiasm

The newly planted wetland at Park Forest will complement a Pennsylvania curriculum standard relating to wetlands.

is contagious." Indeed, it does seem that a critical mass has been achieved, and a variety of new outdoor enhancement projects have been started. I happened to be at the school when excavation was just beginning for the construction of a wetland area right beside the school. Teacher Florence Milutinovic is an enthusiastic promoter of the project and helped to write a unit for the school district that correlates with a Pennsylvania curriculum standard about wetlands. The wetland is being created right outside her classroom window!

Teachers describe a big change at recess. Children are digging and exploring, looking for fossils in the stone wall at one end of the playground, and even coming back after school to dig a little more. Primary teacher Nick Reitz describes how his students formed a nature club on their own at recess, with one girl designing a scavenger hunt at home with pictures of natural items found on the school grounds and little check boxes beside each one. She printed the sheet and brought it in for her classmates to use the next day.

Penn State interns are also a part of these pilot teams. Since most teacher preparation programs include very little formal training concerning schoolyard-enhanced instruction, these undergraduates are gaining a valuable perspective that they will carry throughout their careers. It was encouraging to hear future teachers talk about the need to take children outdoors and provide them with experiences that they may not otherwise receive.

Interns clearly noticed the enthusiasm that their mentor teachers showed when they were working with children outdoors. It was wonderful to hear one intern express that she now sees how nature can be utilized rather than just observed. Without hesitation she gave examples of going outside to do measurement activities or to look for geometric shapes. That's an awareness level that is often difficult even for veteran teachers to see.

"We Chose to Do It"

Donnan Stoicovy provides a wonderful example of how a principal can nurture meaningful staff development. By beginning with the simple schoolyard phenology project, she was able to get classes outside, albeit often for just brief encounters in nature. Those brief excursions, however, frequently ignited an interest in some staff to consider doing more with outdoor learning. By encouraging the formation of the three pilot learning teams, interested teachers had an opportunity to pursue the topic further.

The defining element, however, of the Park Forest professional development program was the fact that learning teams could set their own agendas and areas of focus. As one teacher stressed, "It works so well because we chose to do it." They weren't following detailed prescribed objectives from the office. The principal had truly listened to what her survey results revealed—teachers prefer to learn by discussing information with colleagues.

Chapter 4
Developing Outdoor Learning Programs in Urban Areas

Developing outdoor learning sites in urban areas is not easier or harder than in rural or suburban settings—just different.
Cam Collyer, Evergreen

Because Cam Collyer talked to me early in my tour of school sites, his words often came back to me as I visited schools in diverse settings. I thought about his comment as I visited a schoolyard that is 20 acres in size with a wooded buffer completely surrounding it. The driveway to the school resembles the entrance to a state park. Contrast that with an urban school I toured that was surrounded on three sides by apartment buildings that came within a few feet of the chain-link fence enclosing the schoolyard. Except for the small outdoor classroom area, there was no green space—every square foot was paved. Both sites were being actively used as extensions of the indoor classroom. And, in both cases, teachers and students were very proud of their outdoor learning spaces.

Although the development of outdoor learning spaces in urban areas includes unique challenges, I am also intrigued by the similarities it has with planning for outdoor learning in suburban and rural areas:

- How to encourage more teachers to use the site
- How to facilitate staff development about outdoor learning
- How to maintain the school site
- How to most effectively integrate outdoor instruction into the curriculum
- How to build and maintain administrative support
- How to find and engage volunteers

The list could go on, but you get the idea. For example, teachers in wealthy suburban schools sometimes have as much trouble getting reliable volunteer help as do inner-city schools. In some cases, it's actually easier to get community involvement in a city since schools are usually in the midst of dense population areas where helpers can walk to the site.

In this chapter we first take a look at some of the general challenges of urban schoolyard enhancement and then focus in on the successes of one city's schoolyard enhancement program, the Boston Schoolyard Initiative.

Unique Challenges of Urban Schoolyard Enhancement

Although there are many similar challenges to schoolyard-enhanced learning, it is important to note the unique challenges in an urban setting. Keep in mind that cities differ greatly in terms of how schools are governed, how students are assigned to buildings, and how committed the community is to the concept of green space for both schools as well as the general populace. For example, some cities have been able to assemble enthusiastic private funding collaboratives dedicated to the mission of schoolyard enhancement. These organizations can provide a reliable funding stream that opens opportunities for coordinated planning and the utilization of outside technical and professional resources. Other cities must rely on the voluntary grant-seeking efforts of already busy school personnel if they wish to install outdoor learning elements with a price tag.

Space

The most obvious difference between most rural/suburban schoolyards and urban ones is available space. While most rural/suburban schools are on sites of 10 acres or more (it's not unusual for a suburban elementary school to be on a 15-acre site), most urban schools are planted on much smaller plots. Many older (pre-1950) elementary buildings in most big cities are on sites of 3 acres or less. That sparse acreage has to contain the building, play areas, and parking for staff.

In rural/suburban schools with ample acreage, decisions usually center around what relatively unused space should be converted into learning areas. On a small city lot, however, decisions have to focus on how to rearrange usage patterns or on what activity areas to give up in order to create an outdoor classroom. As a result, urban outdoor classrooms frequently are quite small and compact compared with their rural/suburban counterparts. With careful planning, however, a 2,500-square-foot outdoor learning space can provide a variety of meaningful learning opportunities similar in function to what can be found on a 1-acre site (43,560 square feet). The emphasis is clearly on creating small spaces richly filled with natural materials and equipment that facilitate outdoor instruction.

Shade

Many urban schoolyards have been cleared of trees in order to provide space for play areas and parking. Over the years, much of the green space has been paved, resulting in thousands of square feet of pavement that radiates heat like a stovetop. An outdoor learning area that can provide some shade becomes an oasis in an asphalt desert. Urban schoolyard planners try to incorporate trees and tall shrubs in outdoor classroom spaces to provide both a respite from the sun as well as to create a unique sense of place. In a study of urban schoolyard land cover in Boston, Baltimore, and Detroit, Schulman and Peters (2008) found that the average schoolyard in these cities only had 10 percent tree cover, an amount that they concluded was "very low and inadequate" (73).

Population Density Around the School Site

Although not exclusively an urban factor, most city elementary schools are located in densely populated neighborhoods. When a school is in an area with tightly packed homes, including nearby apartment complexes, there is a high probability that the school site will receive intensive use. Cam Collyer

of Evergreen, a Canadian nonprofit organization that engages Canadians in "sustaining dynamic outdoor spaces—in schools, communities and homes," makes the interesting observation that rural and suburban kids who ride in cars from place to place may sometimes have less contact with the outdoors than city kids who frequently walk to their destinations (Evergreen 2010). The flow of people through an urban school site after school hours and on weekends is usually much greater than in many rural/suburban elementary locations. The challenge for schoolyard enhancers is to add elements to the site that can withstand heavy use and occasional misuse.

Collyer points out that the dense population can actually be a positive factor. With more people, there are more eyes on the site, which can reduce vandalism. The essential ingredient is the establishment of neighborhood pride in the school site. By involving the surrounding neighborhood in planning and maintenance of the site, a caring community can be established that doesn't tolerate vandalism.

A related challenge, faced by rural/suburban as well as city schools, comes from changes in the neighborhood school concept. Increasingly, school districts opt to house students by grade levels rather than by neighborhoods. For example, all students in grades K–3 might be housed in one building and students in grades four to six might be in another, rather than having students in two or three K–6 neighborhood buildings. Often in cities there is busing to magnet schools or other specialized offerings. The many school choices that exist in large cities frequently result in children from any one neighborhood going to several different buildings. One concern expressed by urban school planners is that neighbors may not be as willing to invest time and effort in a schoolyard if their children have no connection to the building.

Parking Concerns

In most rural/suburban schools, parking is not an issue. Because school sites are relatively large, there is plenty of room for a parking lot, with lots of space left over. In large cities, however, parking is a serious issue. Convenient on-street parking is often very difficult to find near most city schools. Parking several streets away is just not an option for teachers who need to lug materials back and forth from their cars, and, depending on the neighborhood, safety concerns may be very relevant.

It's understandable that staff members become concerned when schoolyard enhancers propose taking away parking spaces to install an outdoor classroom.

By keeping the space small, however, it's not necessary to move many cars. One urban planner estimated that five to seven parking spots would provide enough space for an outdoor classroom. Most buildings are able to reconfigure parking (or talk some folks into carpooling!) to make that work.

Turnover of Staff and Administration

Large city districts with dozens of buildings tend to have more movement of teachers and administrators than is typically the case in small rural/suburban districts. Because of sheer size, it is feasible for staff to change buildings and still stay in the same community and district.

However, if administrators change frequently, it can be a challenge to keep the outdoor learning concept in focus. I visited one school recently that had five principals in six years! In high-turnover areas, schools need to have a strong core of teachers who can continue a project even when the administration changes. A school committee that also includes community folks helps to make schoolyard enhancement an expectation rather than an extra.

Kristin Metz of the Boston Schoolyard Initiative points out that the frequent rotation of staff may even have a positive effect. As a principal or teacher leaves a building where there has been a successful outdoor learning program, creative ideas and enthusiasm for schoolyard instruction are carried to the new school.

Controlling Vandalism

Vandalism is certainly not just an urban concern. I have talked with teachers from virtually every type of school demographic, and everyone has stories and concerns about vandalism to outdoor teaching areas. There is no way to "vandal proof" a schoolyard. Indeed, elaborate efforts to keep people out of a space sometimes backfire and are viewed as an inviting challenge to the creative and devious.

Since urban schools are often in densely populated neighborhoods, the schoolyard frequently serves as a common ground for people of many ages. Of course, if there is a lot of unsupervised activity on a site, the possibility for vandalism increases.

Samara Newman of Evergreen, who is also the school ground greening consultant for the Toronto District School Board, has these thoughts concerning vandalism:

- Name it.
- Expect it.
- Clean it up as fast as you can.

That really sums it up well. Vandalism needs to be named and spoken of as a crime. It also is to be expected, however, in an urban landscape with heavy foot traffic. Rapid cleanup of defaced property is essential. Any maintenance person will confirm that graffiti begets more graffiti.

Figure 4.1 This fencing allows potential vandals to see that nothing of great value is stored under the planter and prevents passersby from easily walking through and damaging plantings.

Although some vandalism is inevitable, there are some practical precautions that can be taken. In Boston, soil, planting pots, and inexpensive garden tools are stored in locations that are locked but open to view (see Figure 4.1). The visibility makes it clear that there is nothing of great value being stored. Fences that are low enough to allow the retrieval of objects that fall behind them work well to control damage to fencing. The fencing eliminates easy cut-throughs that can trample plantings. Teachers stress the importance of checking the outdoor classroom for undesirable materials before taking a class outside, especially after a weekend.

The most frequently mentioned antidote for vandalism is neighborhood involvement. Toronto's Samara Newman stresses engaging as many neighborhood stakeholders as possible during the planning of schoolyard enhancements. As an example, she points to signage on several school sites that was created and penned by students, sending a strong message of local involvement.

Some outdoor classroom sites have signs that list the hours of operation, for example, dawn to dusk. Kirk Meyer, former executive director of the Boston Schoolyard Initiative, points out that "since school grounds are public property, this declaration allows police to chase people away who are hanging out at night." He adds that if the police officers who regularly patrol the neighborhood are added to the schoolyard planning group, they may feel an even stronger connection to the site.

All the stakeholders need to stay involved, even after a project is under way or has been completed. There are always things to be maintained in an outdoor learning area. Probably the most important role that neighbors can play is that of vigilant "gatekeepers"—folks who stay alert to what is happening on the site. In most cases, the more eyes watching the site, the less vandalism occurs.

Urban schoolyard planners caution that vandalism varies tremendously by neighborhood, even within central city areas, and even when strong neighborhood involvement efforts are in place. Sometimes the best course of action is to follow Samara's third bit of advice: "Clean it up as fast as you can."

Safety

Concerns about safety are universal. Whether the school is in an affluent suburb or on a street corner in a distressed neighborhood, parents, teachers, and administrators take safety very seriously. To paraphrase Cam Collyer, safety issues in urban areas are not easier or harder than in rural/suburban areas—just different.

It's a fact of urban life that large city school districts will have some neighborhoods that are not as safe as others. As I talked with teachers from schools in relatively high-crime areas, I was struck with both their candor and their pragmatic outlook. Although well aware of crime in the neighborhood, these teachers just kept a watchful eye on their surroundings and confined their students to a clearly delineated area, always aware of the best way to get back into the school quickly if necessary. Basic safety equipment like cell phones and walkie-talkies are also utilized.

Teachers emphasized the value of keeping outdoor study sites small, well defined, and near the building. Like all good teachers, they had accurate knowledge of their surroundings and a "sixth sense" that kicked in if anything seemed abnormal. Although very aware of the need to keep children safe, these teachers also were primarily extolling the value of being able to share nature with their students and get them to go outside and explore.

Collaborative Agreements

Since large city school districts may have hundreds of school buildings, some type of unified or collaborative effort is needed to efficiently marshal

resources and channel schoolyard refurbishing efforts into a comprehensive and systemic approach. It is both cumbersome and an unnecessary duplication of effort for individual buildings in a large urban district to seek project funding on their own.

Urban schoolyard greening projects frequently include an extensive refurbishing of the entire schoolyard, including both play areas and outdoor learning spaces. The projects are viewed as a way to give the entire schoolyard a new and more inviting look. Since old materials need to be removed and new materials and equipment purchased, these projects can become expensive. That's quite different from most rural/suburban outdoor classroom projects, in which usually little needs to be done to the existing play areas or surfaces around the building.

In urban school districts, it is extremely helpful to form collaboratives that can serve as clearinghouses for schoolyard greening efforts. In large cities there are dozens of agencies, neighborhood groups, government offices, and funding organizations that can be brought together to focus efforts systematically on the schoolyard greening effort. The collaborative can facilitate the development of a multiyear plan that makes it easier for organizations to visualize their involvement in the process. Even smaller cities and large county school districts can benefit from the creation of a schoolyard greening collaborative.

The Boston Schoolyard Initiative

I am grateful to the staff of the Boston Schoolyard Initiative (BSI) for much of the information in the following section. The staff graciously shared their experiences, which have spanned fifteen years of schoolyard enhancement efforts in Boston. The longevity of the program has provided many opportunities to try out a variety of approaches to schoolyard improvement. As with any new program, some ideas worked well, while others were modified. The folks at BSI have come up with a model that works well for them but is constantly being reevaluated.

The approach to outdoor learning in Boston differs from that used in many large cities in that it does not focus on gardening as a primary vehicle for outdoor instruction. Since there already are hundreds of excellent books, organizations, and related Web sites that address school gardening, I have chosen to focus on the outdoor classroom concept utilized in Boston. I certainly don't want to minimize school gardening in any way—there are many outstanding programs in urban areas across North America. Rather, I want to provide a look at a lesser-known way of enhancing urban school sites.

The schoolyard enhancement efforts in Boston are supported by a funding collaborative, which has provided the financial resources to secure the talent and materials to implement projects. After touring several schools in Boston, however, I am convinced that many of the enhancements could be duplicated for reasonable cost even in settings that do not have a reliable source of external funding. The following section provides introductory information on the genesis and structure of the BSI. Much of the information in the section is adapted, with permission, from the BSI Web site: www.schoolyards.org.

The Genesis and Structure of the Boston Schoolyard Initiative

The Boston Schoolyard Initiative traces its history to 1994, when the Boston GreenSpace Alliance and the Urban Land Use Task Force approached Mayor Thomas M. Menino to begin a dialogue about the state of Boston's public schoolyards and explore the possibility of a public/private initiative to "revitalize these historically neglected spaces." There was a need to coordinate greening efforts that had already started in the city and to obtain funding for the capital investments that needed to be made on the sites. The mayor convened a Schoolyard Task Force to devise a process for funding and project implementation. The result was the Boston Schoolyard Initiative (BSI), which was officially launched in 1995.

Thanks to the mayor's enthusiastic support, the city has contributed substantially to BSI, especially by funding capital improvements on school sites. Aid from the private sector has also been critical to Boston's success. The Boston Schoolyard Funders Collaborative was established to encourage and oversee private sector involvement in BSI. Working through the Boston Foundation, the Collaborative serves as the central application site for schools submitting proposals for funding.

The Boston Schoolyard Initiative provides grants for two types of projects: schoolyards and outdoor classrooms. The schoolyard makeover is a complete redo of the area surrounding the school, which usually includes replacement of hardscapes as well as the installation of new play equipment. Frequently graphics such as maps or educational games are incorporated into the new surfaces. A school that requests a schoolyard grant also receives an outdoor classroom space. Some schools, however, only apply for an outdoor classroom grant. The outdoor classrooms are relatively small spaces on the school grounds that incorporate a carefully selected array of learning elements, both natural and man-made.

BSI is the critical coordinating arm that brings together teachers, administrators, designers, government, and funders. Because schoolyard improvement is being systemically coordinated by BSI, there is a wonderful opportunity to learn quickly from both successes and snags, and to share information quickly. The fact that BSI has only had two executive directors in fifteen years, and has been working with the same mayor over its entire existence, certainly explains much of the stability and success of the organization.

Figure 4.2 This outdoor classroom at the Gardner Pilot Academy in the Boston neighborhood of Allston is a good example of the variety of plants and enhancements included in BSI projects.

Outdoor Classrooms

After several years of trying schoolyard gardens, Boston chose not to use traditional garden plots as the major elements in its schoolyard enhancement initiative. Regular maintenance of border plantings and garden plots had become a serious concern, and regular classroom usage of the garden areas was just not happening. Consequently, the decision was made to create outdoor classrooms rather than garden spaces.

These relatively small spaces often are about 2,500 square feet and are carefully filled with a wide variety of plants and enhancements (see Figure 4.2). For example, small "urban meadows" are created using the types of plants that students would see in the city. Keeping in mind BSI Director of Education Kristin Metz's philosophy that three trees can be a grove, small "urban woodland" areas were also planted. The mounding of earth creates essential variation of the topography in small spaces (see Figure 4.3). In addition, most outdoor classrooms contain a teaching/meeting area, a hands-on experiment area, and a digging zone. A space is often delineated for viewing succession; nothing is planted there, but the small area is allowed to sprout growth on its own.

Figure 4.3 Some of the surface of this BSI outdoor classroom is mounded to create a more natural topography.

Seating and Pathways

Since outdoor classroom areas are small, it's essential to control the flow of foot traffic. Careful attention is given to the placement of pathways to provide circulation throughout the site, and deadends are avoided. Pathways serve a variety of functions:

- Minimize the problem of mud and dirt collecting on students' shoes
- Steer students away from some features and toward others
- Create a sense of place and interest

I'm amazed how students find a sense of adventure and place in a setting that is not much larger than two or three indoor schoolrooms. Kristin tells the story of second grader who wanted her to see a project he was working on at the other end of the path. "Follow me. We have to go through a forest. Are you scared?" he asked sincerely. For him, this short path lined with plantings just a bit taller than he was served as a forest. It's a vivid testimonial to the fact that a schoolyard learning site does not have to be expansive in order to create a strong impact. In fact, children often gravitate more to smaller spaces.

Seating in a small space can be a challenge. BSI has emphasized the idea of dispersed seating within the confines of its outdoor classrooms. Primarily, logs and boulders are used for seating and are placed in a variety of locations on the site. Since the sites are small and enclosed, it is very easy for a teacher to maintain visual contact with a class. There is often a central gathering area,

Figure 4.4 Here, an effective mix of log and boulder elements serve as seats. Notice how both vertical and horizontal logs are used in the same area.

where seating is also composed of boulders and logs (see Figure 4.4).

In the early years of BSI, teachers were asked, "What would you like on the site?" The most frequently mentioned item was amphitheater-style seating. The question asked now is, "How will you use the site?" The responses are very different. Although some amphitheaters were constructed, it became obvious that, although appropriate for some instructional activities, elevated seating spread students out too much and limited interaction. Outdoor conversation areas need to be tight, which is possible with log or boulder seating arranged in a circle all at the same level. Individual learning activities frequently are more effective when students are spread out over the site, seated in small groupings on rocks and boulders.

To Fence or Not to Fence

Fences are more than just wire or wood; they can evoke a spectrum of strong feelings. For some, fences symbolize safety, containment, and closure; for others, they exemplify distance, estrangement, and inaccessibility.

Originally, many of the Boston outdoor learning areas were not fenced. After talking with teachers, however, it became apparent that the outdoor learning spaces needed to be more clearly delineated if they were to be effective. Having plant materials and other outdoor learning enhancements located on an open schoolyard didn't seem to work effectively—it just felt too open.

Fences were erected to create a signature element that said, "This is an outdoor classroom." Many of the fences are short—some only 3 or 4 feet tall (see Figure 4.5). That's actually an advantage when a stray basketball bounces into the outdoor classroom area after school. If the fence were high, it would probably be cut or bent by climbers trying to retrieve the ball. With a low fence, a person can quickly jump over and return the ball to play.

Figure 4.5 This low fence sets the outdoor classroom apart but allows for relatively easy access to avoid fence vandalism after hours.

Figure 4.6 This gate is a wonderful example of an entrance that is both functional and welcoming.

Figure 4.7 Here is another innovative entrance, which combines a tree trunk with milled boards. Notice how the front fence at this school is made of small vertical logs of varying heights, not chain link.

The fences are not provided primarily for security reasons. Instead, they provide a defined space that children recognize as being different from play areas. The enclosed area also aids in classroom management by making it possible for children to wander among the various elements of the outdoor classroom while always being in view of the teacher.

Fences are usually made of a black, vinyl-coated, chain link, often of a slightly smaller gauge than the typical fence link. The vinyl coating softens the look of the fence and aids in making the fence look like part of the site plan rather than as a precautionary add-on.

In addition to the fences, most of the outdoor classrooms have signature gates or entrances. Figures 4.6 through 4.9 show examples of the gates, fences, and overall look of BSI outdoor classrooms.

Figure 4.8 This outdoor classroom at Adams Elementary School in East Boston not only has a view of the Boston skyline but also has an entrance with fencing on top to provide support for future vines.

Figure 4.9 This photo gives a good overview of the outdoor classroom at Trotter Elementary School in the Boston neighborhood of Dorchester. The photo illustrates well many of the features that are integral to outdoor classrooms designed by BSI. The site is close to the school building but is defined by the fence, with an inviting entrance gate. A variety of seating materials, including boulders, blocks, and logs, are placed among the plantings and provide for dispersed seating. Although this outdoor classroom is a bit larger than most, it still allows good visibility of all areas.

Elements That Add Interest and Functionality

A variety of elements are included in Boston's compact outdoor classroom spaces in order to provide as many opportunities for learning as possible. Many of these elements are low cost and provide study options and flexibility for the site.

Weather-Related Elements

Thermometers are placed on several sides of wooden posts, clearly showing the impact of direct sun exposure to temperature (see Figure 4.10). They are placed at varying heights and in several different locations in the outdoor classroom. A simple rain gauge can be fastened to the posts also, with a weather vane to add both a decorative element as well as a prompt to discuss spatial orientation. Sundials are also included at several sites.

Figure 4.10 Thermometers placed on different sides of wooden posts show the impact of sun exposure on temperature readings at Trotter Elementary.

Armatures

Most Boston outdoor classrooms contain what the planners call armatures—an application of

122

the artistic term referring to a framework for supporting the core of sculpture. These are simply posts with elevated beams that provide height for a variety of uses (see Figure 4.11). The beams provide a place to secure equipment and materials. For example, when studying simple machines, the structures are often rigged with pulleys to provide hands-on experiences. The armatures are useful anytime there is a need for some elevation or a place from which to hang materials or even student artistic creations.

Figure 4.11 Notice how the overhead beams in this schoolyard armature are located near a student seating area so that demonstrations can be seen easily.

Raised Student Planting Beds

In a small space, it just isn't practical to have sprawling planting areas that need to be frequently trimmed back. Raised beds keep plantings contained and easy to see and weed. Raised beds also provide an area for students to dig and get up-close experiences with plants and dirt (see Figure 4.12a–b). If there is any concern about possible contamination from existing soil on the grounds (e.g., from lead or other chemicals), raised planting beds are an excellent choice since safe soil can be used to fill the boxes.

Figure 4.12a–b Raised planting beds like these make it easy for children to gather around a plot to tend plantings or discuss what is growing.

Figure 4.13 Otis Elementary in East Boston has a raised planting bed with a removable wooden panel in front. Although it is not obvious in this photo, there is a plastic window that allows students to see the soil and roots beneath surface when the panel is removed.

Figure 4.14 This raised bed contains plants that are used in rooftop plantings so children can see what might be happening over their heads in the city.

Figure 4.15 For this bulletin board, the school simply included examples of children's writing and drawing based on experiences in the outdoor site, with a few photos included to add interest. The display is not elaborate but certainly conveys the purpose of the outdoor classroom.

Root Observation Door

Some of the raised planting beds in Boston have root observation doors—plastic windows that allow children to see what's happening underground. A wooden panel protects the plastic when not in use (see Figure 4.13). It is a simple idea but can provide a lot of interesting observations and discussion.

Green Roof Simulation

The concept of turning hot city roofs into green areas is growing in popularity. In order to help children better understand the concept, BSI has begun including some raised beds showing the types of plants that are frequently used in rooftop plantings (see Figure 4.14). Plants that grow on rooftops need to withstand extreme temperatures and weather fluctuations. Since watering is not easily done on a rooftop, drought-tolerant plants are also preferred. The green roof simulation is a great example of how the outdoor classroom is helping children learn more about what is happening in their city environment.

Bulletin Boards/Signage

Although they are not unique to urban outdoor classrooms, bulletin boards can provide a way to interpret the area for the neighborhood. Since urban schoolyards often have heavy neighborhood traffic, bulletin boards and interpretive signage may broaden the impact of the outdoor classroom area (see Figures 4.15 and 4.16). One effective signage element is a simple diagram of the outdoor classroom showing the types of plantings and study areas that have been created. Even a basic sign that designates the area as an outdoor classroom is useful. Whether in an urban or a rural setting, it's worthwhile to use every opportunity to explain the purpose and function of outdoor learning sites.

Worktables

Raised space is helpful for sorting, arranging, or organizing materials and equipment (see Figure 4.17). A sturdy table with raised edges is a must in small space.

The Critical Elements

Although it may be possible to locate funding for a variety of site enhancements, building an outdoor classroom is not a guarantee that outdoor education will become an integral part of the curriculum. BSI Director of Education Kristin Metz emphasizes that the Boston Schoolyard Initiative works "very closely with principals, teachers, and the school district to offer professional development opportunities." A part of that process involves bringing teachers together to learn from one another and to share ways to use curriculum support materials.

According to Metz, the Boston Schoolyard Initiative provides three types of professional development training:

1. An introduction to teaching in the outdoor classroom and schoolyard (including behavior management and structuring the lesson to support student learning)

2. "Getting to know" the schoolyard—its plants, animals, rocks, and minerals—for schools with newly constructed BSI schoolyards and outdoor classrooms

Figure 4.16 Simple interpretive signage can be effective. This example explains that a nearby tree trunk is from a tree in Boston and then goes on to describe decomposition. The sign is just heavy laminated paper attached to the fence—not expensive or difficult to replace.

Figure 4.17 This large worktable provides a space for working with materials in the outdoor classroom. Its raised edges keep materials like soil and pebbles contained.

3. Training in two BSI programs that help teachers use the outdoors to directly support the specific requirements of the Boston Public Schools curriculum and related content: Science in the Schoolyard and Outdoor Writers Workshop

Kristin explains that, for schools receiving Capital Construction Grants for outdoor classrooms or larger schoolyard improvement initiatives (including play areas), there are very specific professional development requirements. Schools receiving an outdoor classroom commit to four to ten hours of professional development in the first year following completion of the outdoor classroom, with strong encouragement to continue professional development in the second year. Additional professional development is available by arrangement, and strongly encouraged in the following year, and consists of a combination of after-school training and support during the school day. For teachers who are interested in deepening their content knowledge, BSI offers courses district-wide for inservice credit. These are available to any teacher in the district independent of whether they have a BSI outdoor classroom.

Professional development, peer support, and help in aligning outdoor instruction to the curriculum are truly the critical elements in a successful outdoor learning program. It really doesn't matter whether the program is in a rural district in Georgia or in downtown Boston—the availability of collegial support and instructional expertise is just as important as the physical space provided and the site enhancements that have been added.

The Urban Schoolyard Greening Movement

For many years, urban schoolyards were stereotyped as asphalt deserts, similar to prison yards, designed primarily for surveillance and exercise (Allen 1968). That dismal perception is changing, however, as cities increasingly explore ways to partner with community groups, agencies, and boards of education to create more positive schoolyard environments.

The interest in greening urban schoolyards certainly has been fueled by a growing body of research that points strongly to the positive effects of schoolyard enhancement in general and outdoor learning in particular. The early research of Gerald Lieberman and Linda Hoody (1998) showed the positive academic and attitudinal impact of using the environment as an integrating context for learning and sparked an interest in further research about outdoor learning.

Although relatively few research studies looked at the impact of place on learning prior to 1998, the topic is big today. The Place-Based Education Evaluation Collaborative (2011) lists more than 120 research studies related to place-based education between 2004 and mid-2009. Although place-based education is broader than just the use of the schoolyard for instruction, even a quick reading of the list shows the keen interest that exists in exploring the impact of education that goes beyond the traditional classroom.

Another organization that is providing an excellent clearinghouse for exploring research about children and the outdoors is the Children and Nature Network (2011). This organization provides a synthesis of research studies with links to dozens of current outdoor-related research projects. The Web site (www.childrenandnature.org/research) includes summaries of research reports, citation details, and information about each document's availability. In many cases you can go directly to the full study from the Web site.

As the research continues to show the benefits of outdoor experiences for children, a number of large cities from coast to coast have chosen to take schoolyard greening very seriously, with *schoolyard* usually defined as all of the land surrounding a school building, not just play areas. Kirk Meyer is the former (and founding) executive director of the Boston Schoolyard Initiative. Currently, he is the executive director of the Green Schoolyard Network (http://greenschoolyardnetwork.org), an organization dedicated to transforming schoolyards into dynamic centers for teaching and learning, health and fitness, environmental literacy, and community life in the United States. Kirk has compiled a representative listing of some of the large urban areas that have schoolyard initiatives in place (Meyer 2010). In addition to the Boston Schoolyard Initiative, Kirk mentions the following:

The San Francisco Green Schoolyard Alliance (www.sfgreenschools .org). This organization serves children and families of San Francisco by "promoting and supporting green schoolyards." The alliance provides "resources, training, and advocacy to school communities to help them create and sustain outdoor learning environments" (SFGSA).

Learning Landscapes (Denver, Colorado) (www.ucdenver.edu/academics/ colleges/ArchitecturePlanning/discover/centers/CCCD/LearningLandscapes).

"Since 1998, through a successful collaboration between multiple stakeholders, the Learning Landscapes initiative has transformed fifty-six neglected Denver public elementary school playgrounds into attractive and safe multiuse parks tailored to the needs and desires of the local community" (Meyer 2010).

The Greening of Detroit (www.greeningofdetroit.com). "The Greening of Detroit works with dozens of schools throughout the City of Detroit, planting trees to beautify children's schoolyards, and teaching children how to become stewards of their environment" (Meyer 2010).

Trust for Public Land (New York City) (www.tpl.org/tier2_rl.cfm?folder_id=631). The Trust's efforts are a part of Mayor Bloomberg's PlaNYC2030. This program plans to create more than 200 acres of new parkland on 185 schoolyards (Meyer 2010).

Washington, D.C., Environmental Education Consortium (www.dcschoolyardgreening.org). The mission of the D.C. Environmental Education Consortium's Schoolyard Greening program is to "increase and improve schoolyard green spaces to promote ecological literacy and environmental stewardship among students, teachers, parents and the surrounding community" (D.C. Environmental Education Consortium 2010).

First Hand Learning (Buffalo, New York) (www.firsthandlearning.org). According to Director of Publications Kristen Gasser, "First Hand Learning is a nonprofit organization that works with school districts, informal education providers, and businesses to design and implement curriculum materials and professional development programs that emphasize direct, firsthand experiences with natural, technological, and cultural phenomena. Now in its third printing, *Outdoor Inquiries: Taking Science Investigations Outside the Classroom* is available at FHL's Web site, where materials lists, mini-journals, and sample lessons may be downloaded for free."

REAL School Gardens (Fort Worth, Texas) (www.realschoolgardens.org). "REAL School Gardens partners with elementary school communities to create learning gardens that raise hope, spark imaginations and connect children to nature" (Meyer 2010).

SPARK (Houston, Texas) (www.sparkpark.org). SPARK was initiated in 1983 with the goal of increasing park space in Houston. To become involved, a school's principal sends SPARK a letter of interest "describing the school and its needs. If selected, the principal forms a SPARK Committee that works with a landscape architect to design a park that will be open to the neighborhood after school and on the weekends" (Meyer 2010).

Meyer also points out that the schoolyard greening movement is international in scope. National organizations that place a strong emphasis on schoolyard enhancement are in place in the United Kingdom, Canada, Sweden, Norway, and Australia.

* * * * * *

Currently, "green is good" has become a national slogan. The popularity of all things environmental makes it a bit easier than in previous decades to encourage a rethinking of urban schoolyards. Although urban schoolyard greening presents complex challenges, it's wonderful to see how many large cities are embracing the concept. For those who want to go beyond slogans and see proof that green space is worth the effort, please take a careful look at the Children and Nature Network (C&NN) "Research and Publications" section. C&NN has made a tremendous contribution to our understanding of children and the outdoors by summarizing research studies from 2007 to the present (www.childrenandnature.org). Even a quick scanning of the research summaries shows quite consistently that children and adults benefit from contact with nature.

Spotlight 4
Principals Are the Key

It's really a symbiotic relationship: If schoolyard-enhanced learning is going to work, there has to be a strong interdependence between teachers and administrators. Both need to be sold on the value of outdoor learning, and both need to work together to generate resources and enthusiasm. Teachers who use outdoor learning are very quick to mention that strong administrative support is essential, even for small outdoor learning programs.

The two principals described in this spotlight illustrate the attitudes and approaches used by so many administrators that I met during my travels for this book. Toni Hill and Fritz Monroe have somewhat different styles, but both successfully achieve the same goal: helping teachers use the outdoors as an instructional tool.

Meet Toni Hill

Forest View Elementary is a K–5 building in Durham, North Carolina, that serves more than 600 students. Teachers are proud of the outdoor learning enhancements that have been made to their site and frequently mention the efforts of retired founding principal Toni Hill.

Toni had recently completed her doctorate and was a strong advocate of constructivist learning when she became the founding principal of Forest View in 1993. She served the school until retiring in 2005,

Toni Hill, former principal of Forest View Elementary in Durham, North Carolina

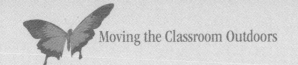

always passionately promoting the philosophy that nothing can make learning more real than going outside. As Toni says, "When you have students outside—observing, planting gardens, watching birds, fishing—those children in their adult lives have a greater sense of stewardship. They become better learners also because they internalize what they are learning."

Encouragement

Toni's strong advocacy for outdoor learning was fostered during her doctoral work at Columbia. Discussions about constructivism convinced Toni that as an administrator she needed to help teachers make learning relevant and real for children. She knew that staff members who also were interested in making the outdoors part of their classrooms needed to be encouraged. Toni modestly says that it was easy to find support for her philosophy because the school was already full of teacher leaders; she just followed them. Toni feels that her greatest contribution

Flowers, vegetables, birdhouses, and art greet visitors at the entrance to Forest View Elementary.

was to readily say, "Oh, that *is* a great idea. Let's do it! Let's see how we can find money." Current teachers who worked with Toni emphasize that she has a marvelous understanding of what it means to empower teachers.

A basic problem that Toni recognized very quickly was that teachers became excited about a project, but when they could not find resources they became discouraged. She was determined to empower her staff and support their ideas so that they would have confidence to look for resources that they needed to get projects off the ground.

Empowerment Through Grant Writing

One way that she empowered her staff was to make available building-level grant funding. Working with the school's parent/teacher association, money from PTA fund-raisers could be accessed through easy-to-write grant proposals. If teachers wrote grants together, larger amounts were awarded. By making it relatively easy to receive a small local grant, teachers gained the confidence to apply for larger funding at the district and community level. Toni was always careful to route potential grant possibilities around the building. The grants were evaluated by the parents, teachers, and community members as needed.

Toni remembers finding an announcement in the mail about a $50,000 grant opportunity offered by a national corporation. Although it was a long shot, she sent the grant on to a teacher who had been successful with small local grants. To everyone's delight, Forest View received the grant and was able to establish a science resource room with equipment and materials to support science instruction throughout the building.

The grant also made it possible to construct outdoor learning centers on the school grounds, which reinforced grade-level outdoor themes. For example, first graders focused on vegetable gardens, so raised beds were included in their outdoor learning center. In second grade the emphasis was on butterflies, with an outdoor learning center that had a butterfly garden as the centerpiece. Weather stations and North Carolina native plant gardens were also incorporated into other outdoor learning centers.

By nurturing grant-writing skills at the building level, Toni established a cadre of people who had the confidence to tackle even complicated funding applications. The teachers writing those grants felt much more empowered, and a greater sense of ownership, than if the grant had been written in Toni's office. It's interesting to note that every grant had to include some money to increase the professional book collection. By the time she retired, the building had developed an excellent resource library using very few district funds.

Test Scores and Authentic Learning

Toni was a principal during the years when test scores increasingly became viewed as the key measures of a school's "success." In her very matter-of-fact way, she said that her philosophy was to "keep test scores high enough so people would leave us alone to do what was right for children!" She feels that as people turn away from hands-on learning, then test scores drop. The reason, she says, is because students often do not internalize what they are being taught.

Former teacher Bob Palmatier worked at Forest View as a science facilitator from the time that Toni opened the building. He echoes Toni's emphasis upon authentic learning. "Kids become excited when they have the opportunity to become scientists—to do the behaviors of scientists. Kids become excited when they make discoveries—when they see patterns in data that they have observed over time. That's what real scientists do." Although content is important, Toni understands that that process skills provide the key to authentic learning. By engaging in process skills like observing, recording, and inferring, students are doing what scientists do. She made it her mission to empower her staff to focus on what really matters.

Meet Fritz Monroe

Fritz Monroe, principal of Brookside Elementary in Worthington, Ohio

"He's been missing for a few days," Fritz Monroe remarked casually as I looked into a terrarium in his office. The terrarium had recently been home to a small ball python. Without a pause, Fritz eagerly continued his description of the sixth-grade ancient civilizations unit in which students tried (unsuccessfully) to make fire with steel, flint, and dryer lint.

Fritz has been the principal at Brookside Elementary, a K–6 building with about 320 students in Worthington, Ohio, for about twenty years. Although Worthington is usually viewed as an upper-income community bordering Columbus, Brookside serves a diverse population, with nearly one-third of its students participating in the free- and reduced-lunch program. The school is located on 8.5 acres in a quiet suburban neighborhood.

Providing Infrastructure for Outdoor Learning

Fritz has always been convinced that outdoor learning is a powerful tool. He also firmly believes that it is his responsibility to create an infrastructure that facilitates outdoor teaching. Early in his tenure at Brookside, he saw the potential of using a storm-water retention basin on a corner of the school site as a pond. Although the retention pond still collected and dispersed water as originally intended, it now was also viewed as a teaching resource. Over the years he added an outdoor seating area near the pond as well as a wonderful observation deck that extends over the water and also serves as a teaching space. Turtles sunning on a log on a warm day in May are wonderful indicators of the rich habitat that exists around the pond. The two teaching/meeting areas and the pond's close proximity to the building make it a very usable and accessible resource for teachers.

Part of the Brookside outdoor teaching infrastructure is a teaching/meeting area that extends over the pond.

For many of his years at Brookside, Fritz took a low-key approach to outdoor learning. He encouraged people to go outside and talked with teachers about what a natural fit it was to use outdoor learning, but really didn't launch a formal "initiative." It should be noted that for many years the district also had a formal, centralized outdoor education program, which reinforced the importance of outdoor learning and provided a variety of learning experiences and resources for all classrooms in the district. As financial pressures caused the formal district outdoor education program to fade, Fritz realized that it was important to begin a more formalized outdoor learning focus in his building.

Outdoor Learning as the Context

In 2006, the district began an initiative emphasizing twenty-first-century learning skills. Schools were expected to develop proposals for renewal projects that would meet building-specific needs. Fritz convened faculty, staff, and parents for input. After considering parent input, staff interests, and the site configuration, the decision was made to focus on schoolyard-enhanced learning as a guiding structure for renewal. Although there was general agreement that outdoor/ experiential learning was valuable for all students, there also was consensus that schoolyard-enhanced learning could provide valuable concrete experiences for the lower-income population that made up over one-third of the student body. As Fritz notes, "Ruby Payne's [2005] work with children in poverty points to how important concrete experiences, and the following engagement with teachers, is to the education and development of impoverished children."

The focus of the Brookside effort is to use outdoor learning as a context for developing skills such as communication, use of technology, working in teams toward specific goals, problem solving, critical thinking, and shared decision making (Brookside Elementary School 2008). In a nutshell, Brookside wants to develop a student population that is proficient at gathering data, interpreting data, and presenting findings.

With the renewal effort in focus, Fritz has stepped up his efforts to provide the "infrastructure" for outdoor learning:

- A butterfly garden (in the shape of a butterfly) has been planted.
- A school vegetable garden plot that has a wedge-shaped chunk for every grade level has been established. The garden is being done cooperatively with the community, which provides labor, especially in the summer.
- "Learning stumps" (a student came up with the name) have been created from a downed tree and form a teaching/meeting area near the building.
- A small orchard has been started through the national Fruit Tree Planting Foundation (http://www.ftpf.org).
- A land compass is being installed to show the movement of the sun. Markings will also be included to show directionality.

Wedge-shaped plots delineate classroom gardens.

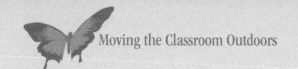

An emphasis on the outdoors occurs inside also. Brookside was built during the era when courtyards were popular. Bird feeders are set up in one courtyard, and students can observe them using an indoor bird blind made by taping paper over glass windows, with just a small slit of the windows exposed.

Another interior courtyard has an area for tortoises to roam during suitable temperatures. The animals are visible from the hallway and provide a constant source of interest. On the other side of the hallway, a small tank is home to some tadpoles that will eventually end up in the pond.

Fritz tries to provide an infrastructure for outdoor learning as well as encouragement. Students recognize and appreciate his love of the outdoors. As I was meeting with Fritz, two students excitedly came in with what they thought were monarch eggs and asked Mr. Monroe for his opinion—a beautiful example of a principal who is obviously considered to be an approachable person as well as a local nature expert. He proudly introduced me to teachers who were using the outdoors and asked them to tell me about their projects. Not only did I learn what was happening at Brookside, but teachers were affirmed by being able to tell their own stories.

Chapter 5
Enhancing Outdoor Learning with Technology
Matthew Broda

Right after winter break, Mrs. Garcia began making preparations for her sixth-grade students to participate in a long-range integrated curriculum project. The project would incorporate a variety of technological elements into the study of the migratory behavior of a schoolyard favorite: the American robin. During the first half of the year, Mrs. Garcia had noticed the interest her students were showing in the robin that frequented their schoolyard. Students also questioned where the robin went during the winter and when they could expect to see the bird again in the spring.

During the winter break, Mrs. Garcia had discovered the Journey North Web site (www.learner.org/jnorth/) created by Annenberg Media. Journey North provides students and teachers with the opportunity to act as researchers from their own schoolyards by tracking the migratory progress and patterns of a wide range of species. With the help of the Journey North site, Mrs. Garcia's students would be able to develop their observational and descriptive skills in their own schoolyard while contributing to a project that connected their class to a larger community.

Mrs. Garcia realized that this project was going to need some structure in order for her students to get the most out of the experience. The PTA had raised money to build a bird blind on the school grounds, and Mrs. Garcia was excited to put it to use as quickly as possible. This blind would provide

students with an official research station in which they could develop their observational skills. But while these observational skills were important, Mrs. Garcia also wanted to integrate research, writing, collaborative work, and the use of other critical twenty-first-century skills into this ongoing project. To do this she developed three distinct phases for the unit and aligned the project objectives with specific technological applications that could enhance the students' outdoor experiences.

For Phase I, Mrs. Garcia identified research skills, map skills, and the development of predictions and hypotheses as her main instructional objectives. To accomplish these objectives, she chose three technologies to implement: (1) the development of a class wiki, (2) the use of hand-held global positioning system (GPS) machines, and (3) the use of Google Earth. During the winter months, the class wiki would be used as a central location for the research collected and the predictions made by the students about the American robin (for more about wikis, see page 151). The public nature of the wiki also broadened the audience for the students' work beyond the walls of the classroom—their work could be viewed all over the world! The GPS machines and Google Earth would be used together to develop map skills as well as spatial awareness of their own school grounds. As spring approached, Mrs. Garcia felt that her students would be prepared for Phase II.

In Phase II, Mrs. Garcia wanted students to spend time outside observing and collecting data from the schoolyard habitat. While the bird blind would be an important component, she hoped that the students' research would also provide insights as to where on the school grounds they could expect to find the robin. In addition to the observations, she wanted her students to develop networks with other classrooms around the country who were also monitoring the robin. To accomplish these goals, Mrs. Garcia decided to implement three new technologies: (1) Google Docs word processing and spreadsheet programs, (2) a new class blog linked to the class wiki, and (3) the Journey North online databases. Mrs. Garcia's decision to use Google Docs spreadsheets was driven by cost. The classroom computers were outdated and slow when running the school's software, but the Google suite of programs worked much faster and only required a browser and an Internet connection—plus, it was free! In addition, students could record their observational data in a central location without the worry of the data being lost and with the added benefit of being able to access it from any computer.

Although the class wiki was a great place for reporting, Mrs. Garcia wanted her class to engage and interact with other classes. A class blog would allow for conversations. Finally, the Journey North site had a user-friendly system for classes to supply their observational data about robins into the huge pool of data being collected from around the country. Students could see how their efforts would impact the larger project. With these technologies, she was confident that her students would have a rich and meaningful experience. To ensure lasting impact, Mrs. Garcia developed a third phase for the project, which would focus on reflection and the development of new ideas.

In Phase III, Mrs. Garcia wanted her students to synthesize and evaluate their exploration of bird behavior. She wanted them to work in collaborative teams to develop new understandings, and she wanted to provide them with meaningful and authentic means to convey these new understandings. To facilitate these goals, Mrs. Garcia gave students three choices: (1) podcasting, (2) digital stories, and (3) Google Docs. Podcasting provided students with the opportunity to tell their stories through sound alone. Digital stories allowed students to combine both visual and audio elements into their storytelling. Both of these mediums required students to work in collaborative teams, develop new skills using software, and create ways to convey their messages beyond text alone. Mrs. Garcia did offer students a more traditional medium with Google Docs word processing, but the students who choose this option were required to use the collaborative writing features to network with another student from a different part of the country.

Now that the project is over, Mrs. Garcia is pleased with her students' success and how deeply they understand the content. She has seen firsthand how truly beneficial technological mediums can be in enhancing outdoor learning.

Outdoor Learning in Three Phases

In reaction to the current digital practices of today's youth, many are advocating a return to the natural world and subsequent limitation of digital consumption. As rates of obesity and attention deficit disorders rise, many are turning a wary eye toward the increased emphasis on all things digital. But does nature have to be at odds with the digital environments that are defining the twenty-first-century classrooms of today? Most important, can

the digital world actually complement the natural/experiential world and vice versa? As we have seen in the vignette above, the answer is an emphatic *yes*!

Whether in an outdoor setting or in the classroom, the difference between the success and failure of a learning experience is dependent on the student's ability to reflect on the experience. The ultimate goal of this reflective process, and the experiential learning process as a whole, is to provide present and future relevance "for the learner and the society in which he/she is a member" (Wurdinger 1997, 4). The purpose of experiential learning is not to develop silos of understanding, but to develop a web that connects past, present, and future learning to real and relevant situations.

This web of connections serves as our tipping point where technology begins to complement outdoor learning experiences. We can look at outdoor learning as a three-phase process (see Figure 5.1).

In Phase I, preexperience, practitioners need to front load the outdoor experience and provide students with opportunities to do the following:

- Build foundational knowledge
- Develop some initial interpretations
- Express and research concerns
- Seek clarity about expectations

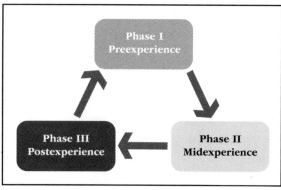

Figure 5.1 Three-Phase Model

Phase I is the time when students are made aware of the knowledge, skills, and dispositions they will be expected to develop throughout the outdoor learning experience. As illustrated through Mrs. Garcia's example at the beginning of the chapter, the development of a class wiki is an effective way for students to begin exploring and reporting about the topic at hand.

In Phase II, midexperience, practitioners need to provide students with the structures and tools necessary for the collection of information. Regardless of the purpose of the outdoor learning, students need to be able to capture the experience in some way, and technological means can be helpful in this endeavor. Through the use of audio, video, and photographic recording devices, students can develop a chronological diary for any given experience and can provide auditory and visual cues for future analysis, evaluation, and reflection. This archive can serve as a critical tool for understanding the changes and learning that occurred throughout the experience.

Finally, in Phase III, postexperience, practitioners need to provide students with opportunities to reflect on, synthesize, and evaluate conclusions; engage in dialogue with others regarding their personal and collective growth; and create new works that express their understanding. To do this, students need to be engaged in collaborative work and provided with meaningful and authentic means to convey these new understandings. Technological media need to be selected that require students to develop new skills using software as well as seek ways to convey their message beyond text alone. Phase III should challenge students to bring their learning full circle through thoughtful analysis, evaluation, and creation.

Technology can complement outdoor learning experiences. By using a phased approach to developing outdoor experiences and then aligning objectives in each phase with supportive technological methodologies, students can gain a much richer and deeper understanding of the curriculum, themselves, their learning community, and the larger world. Supportive technologies for each phase are described in the remainder of this chapter. In addition, descriptions of specific applications to outdoor learning are included in shaded boxes. These examples will help you more easily visualize how to bring these technologies into your own teaching.

Phase I: Preexperience

In Phase I, the preexperience phase, practitioners need to front load, or prepare the students for the outdoor experience. Front loading provides students with an opportunity to build foundational knowledge, make connections to previous learning, develop initial interpretations, express and research concerns, and seek clarity about expectations. As a teacher, this is the time when your students are made aware of the knowledge, skills, and dispositions they will be expected to develop throughout the experience. Obviously, a critical phase! But what will the students actually *do* during this phase? How can technology enhance this process? We provide answers to these questions in the following sections.

Terminology and Cautions

In Phase I, students gather and process new information in order to develop a wide base from which further inquiry can occur. Because the bulk of the

content discussed in this phase, as well as in other phases, will rely heavily on the use of Web 2.0 and cloud computing technologies, it's important to have an understanding of these two terms. In addition, it's important to educate yourself and your students on Internet safety; cyber-awareness is essential for all teachers and their students who use technology.

Web 2.0

Web 2.0 is the new generation in Web interaction. For the most part, the Internet had been a place where people went to get information—a one-way street. Think of this as Web 1.0—the first version. With these terms we are not talking about software, but rather how you use the Internet. Where Web 1.0 was a one-way street, Web 2.0 is two-way. It is a principle that is moving the Internet from a place where you passively receive content to a place where you are actually creating and interacting with the content—a give-and-take exchange of ideas and information.

A familiar and powerful example of Web 2.0 is Wikipedia (www.wikipedia .org). Wikipedia, an online encyclopedia, allows users to participate in the authoring process as an effort to keep the content as up-to-date as possible. As its name suggests, Wikipedia is built in a structure known as a wiki, or a collaborative Web-authoring interface. People can now both receive and create content. Sure, this process of collaborative and public authoring presents some issues (people writing about content they don't know, intentional incorrect content, etc.), but it also provides some amazing opportunities for changing the Web experience. While issues may arise, you also need to remember that the world can observe, moderate, and correct issues as they happen—at times with more accuracy and speed than conventional methods.

Cloud Computing

Web 2.0 has allowed for the development of a new space for delivering computer applications and services. The cloud simply refers to the Internet. Because Web 2.0 enables people to add content to the Internet, it is conceivable that many of the applications—word processing software, photo editing software, and so on—that used to "live" on every computer could now live in the "cloud," on the Internet, for all to use.

Word processing is a good example. When using Microsoft Word, you are, for the most part, creating content in a way that is similar to creating a simple

Web page or adding content to a wiki as described above. Web 2.0 design allows you to do the same type of work you are doing on your computer-based word processing application, but over the Internet. The benefits to this type of platform are numerous:

- You can access your work from anywhere, eliminating the need for schools to buy multiple copies of an application that can only be installed on certain machines. If you have a computer and Internet access, you are connected.
- While some cloud applications do require a membership fee, the vast majority have free options for users.
- Cloud computing allows for highly portable content. The content resides in the cloud—accessible from any Internet-connected computer.
- Collaboration, sharing, and publishing processes are simplified. Many applications are set up so that multiple users can work on the same content at the same time from multiple locations. Students can connect with experts and peers beyond the classroom walls.

Cyber-Awareness

It is essential to discuss some cautions to keep in mind when using both Web 2.0 and cloud technologies. Students and teachers need to be alert and safety-conscious when working in online environments. Make sure you establish ground rules and expectations for online dialogue to prevent cyber-bullying and contact with cyber-predators.

All school districts are required to have well-established policies that govern the use of Internet technology, so it is important to alert the district of your plans to use Web 2.0 technologies and to investigate the policies thoroughly. District technology policies are required in order to be in compliance with the following laws (FCC 2011; FTC 2011)

- The Children's Internet Protection Act (CIPA). Web site: www.fcc.gov/cgb/consumerfacts/cipa.html
- The Children's Online Privacy Protection Act (COPPA). Web site: www.coppa.org/comply.htm

It is very important that you get to know these pieces of legislation and find the person in your school or district who is the resident expert. Student use of online resources must comply with district policies and the two legislative acts mentioned above.

Many parents have negative reactions to online learning experiences because of the well-publicized dangers that exist, but there is also an enormous amount of compelling and educational content that students can access safely with the proper precautions in place. As a teacher, it is critical that your voice is heard in conversations about Internet safety so that you can show the aspects of online technologies that will engage and prepare children for a successful future, while working in a safe environment.

The bulk of the technologies featured later in this chapter use Web 2.0 and cloud-based applications that require users to go through a sign-up process to access services. These sign-up processes are at the heart of COPPA. To protect your students and yourself, I advise that you do the following for each online application you choose to use:

1. Read the "Terms of Service" that you are required to accept when joining or subscribing to a service. These agreements contain valuable information, such as required age limits and the ability to use a master account for multiple students who do not meet the age requirements.

2. For students under the age of 13 (I suggest under the age of 18), obtain "verifiable parental consent" (i.e., a permission slip) for the use of all online technologies. In your permission slip, provide a detailed description of the service and how the students will be using the service in class. Instead of just using a permission slip, many teachers request that the child's parent or guardian create the necessary online accounts so that there is no mistaking what the online service is and what is expected.

3. Use a single classroom user account when possible. Many times this single account will work for what you will want to do. Create an account for yourself and then add content created by your students.

4. Use linked e-mail accounts. For certain services that require an e-mail address, teachers can use an existing Gmail account—or set up a new one—and create a number of e-mail addresses that are all linked to the main address. As Kim Cofino describes on her technology blog, "Basically, this means that one teacher can have 20 permanent e-mail accounts that are all delivered into one teacher e-mail account" (Cofino 2007). This eliminates the possibility that students will receive any e-mail as a result of signing up for the service, but each student will still have a unique login address.

5. Join the service through a paid educational pricing account. While it may cost a small amount to do, these educational accounts are designed to meet all of the CIPA and COPPA regulations to ensure that you are in compliance. Most educational pricing accounts remove unwanted advertising.

6. Make sure you understand your district policies governing the posting of student work and images. Usually, this will require you to make sure the parents or guardians fill out the necessary forms.

Tools for Retrieving, Recognizing, and Recalling

Much of the work done by students in Phase I will be focused on the retrieval, recognition, and recollection of information. For the most part, these processes will be enhanced through the use of Web search engines, social bookmarking, Web-based note-taking systems, and Really Simple Syndication (RSS). While each of these technologies may also be beneficial during other stages of an outdoor learning experience, we will look at using these technologies to front load, or prepare, the students.

Search Engines

Search engines are the most frequently used tool for most online computer users, especially your students. Frequently, students are aware of the search process (ask your students if they have ever "Googled" anything) but are not versed in how to yield the best results when searching. Students preparing for an outdoor learning experience need to develop the skills necessary to retrieve, recognize, and recall quality information.

To help provide their users with the most comprehensive search results, most search engine companies provide detailed instructions on how to conduct searches. For example, the most familiar search engine, Google, provides the following guidelines (Google 2011) for developing your search terms:

- *Keep it simple.*
- *Think about how the page you are looking for will be written.*
- *Use the words that are most likely to appear on the page.* For example, instead of "how things change in nature over time," use "phenology"
- *Describe what you need with as few terms as possible.* For example, "trillium" will give better results than "forest floor flowers."
- *Choose descriptive words.* For example, "North Dakota robin" is more descriptive than "robin."

By following these simple searching suggestions, students can move beyond simply "Googling" a topic, to conducting focused and well-reasoned research.

Outdoor Learning Application: Search Engines

In one fourth-grade classroom, a teacher was preparing her students to use their class garden as a catalyst for developing haiku poems about nature. Students in the class were divided into teams that researched the various types of plants found in the garden. Groups paid particular attention to specific scientific content about the plants, such as scientific name and classification, territorial range, physical structure, and so on.

On the first day of research, student teams were assigned the same plant, but different search engines. For the teacher, the research was not so much the content the students found for the same plant, but rather a comparison of the various search engines and the results they received from each. Students developed a Venn diagram that compared the search engines used. These comparisons included topics such as ease of use, search method, and presentation of search results. By the end of the class, students had begun to develop an awareness of how the search engines differed and how certain engines could be beneficial when researching various topics for outdoor learning.

Social Bookmarking

Social bookmarking helps direct students in their searching efforts and helps them develop collaborative lists of Web sites that relate to specific topics. Social bookmarking takes the familiar task of bookmarking favorite Web pages, typically done in a browser and stored on an individual computer, and moves it into the cloud, where the bookmarks can be accessed from anywhere and shared with other people. One of the most popular social bookmarking sites today is Delicious (www.delicious.com), a site sponsored by Yahoo!. Delicious allows users to host categorized collections of bookmarks and creates a Web page that lists all of your bookmarks so that you can share it with other people. You can even create a compilation of bookmarks collected from different people.

It is easy to imagine that you could end up with a very long list of bookmarks when using this type of service. Students need to be able to access the bookmarks most important to them—quickly! Enter "tagging." Every site you choose to bookmark can be labeled, or tagged, with key words. These tags will allow students to just look at just the sites that match the tag word they enter. Tagging is a great way to make a huge list of links searchable and organized.

While there are a number of Web sites that provide similar bookmarking services, Delicious has proved to be one of the most user friendly for students of all ages. When used in conjunction with the searching practices described in the preceding section, social bookmarking can add considerable value to the preexperience phase.

Outdoor Learning Application: Social Bookmarking

Let's go back to our fourth-grade class preparing for their nature-based haiku experience. Once the teacher had established some background knowledge for how to search, the students went off and began their searches in earnest, focusing on the variety of plants they had in their class garden. Students developed a uniform list of tags that they would use to help categorize all of the pertinent Web pages they found. Students used multiple tags for some pages. For example, one student found a page that was helpful in understanding the daffodil, and it also contained the habitat range. Because of this, the student tagged the page "daffodil" and "habitat." By doing this, the class could look at all of the pages related to the daffodil, but they could also sort out all of the pages that dealt with the habitat ranges for all of the plants in the garden.

Web Notes

The use of Web notes is a cloud-based approach for collecting and compiling all of the information students find online. There are a number of programs that help online users take notes (Notefish, Yahoo!, Notepad, Springnote, Notezz, Zotero, etc.), but one of the simplest applications is Evernote .com (www.evernote.com). Evernote.com is a free online membership service (paid options are available if you want more storage space and no ads)

that allows you to capture specific aspects of Web pages as clips that can be shared, organized, and, most important, traced back to the original source. This last feature is what truly sets this type of system apart from simply having students copy and paste online content from the Internet to a word processing document. Every clip that is saved is directly linked to the original page. Clips can also be tagged using the same tags discussed in the preceding section on social bookmarking so that students can sort and search through their content.

Outdoor Learning Application: Web Notes

For our class preparing for a haiku project, the teacher has guided her students through a process of locating and tagging Web pages that pertained to the plants selected. The students followed this work with beginning the process of culling the content to highlight the most useful and important information.

Using the tags as their guides, and the clipping feature of their Web note program, the students went back through their collected Web pages and made focused "clips" of the content found on each page. Students applied the appropriate tags to each of their clips for easy future reference. As students came across content that was beneficial to their classmates, they shared their clips with each other with a click of the mouse. By the end of the process, students had distilled the most pertinent information from each page into a collaborative collection of organized notes—still linked to the original sources.

Really Simple Syndication (RSS)

The information your students are seeking to learn related to an outdoor learning experience may change frequently, or students may find a particular source that provides regular, current content. In the latter situation, Really Simple Syndication (sometimes known as Rich Site Summary), or RSS, can be helpful. RSS allows you to subscribe to a Web page that will then send you notifications about new stories added to the site. Not all Web pages are RSS enabled, so your best bet is to look for the RSS symbol (◼) in the URL window of your browser. Clicking the symbol will open a new page that is simply a list of all the content on the site. You can save this "feed" as a link, or you can use an RSS reader. Reader services are offered through a number of sites, including Bloglines, My Yahoo! (if you have a Yahoo! account), and Google (Google Reader). Many Internet browsers also have RSS reader and subscription functions built right into the interface.

Outdoor Learning Application: RSS

So how can RSS enhance your students' outdoor learning experiences? Many teachers track RSS feeds coming from sources with different viewpoints that pertain to the experiences they are developing for their students. Perhaps you are preparing your students to study the impact of adding a new parking lot on the school grounds. There are a number of agencies and blogging services that would have timely and appropriate information related to land use and its impacts.

A principal in Georgia was developing a presentation for parents about the importance of outdoor learning. By tracking RSS feeds from the Children and Nature Network and the National Wildlife Federation, she was able to get up-to-the-minute information and news releases from highly reliable resources.

Tools for Understanding

Constructing meaning, interpreting, exemplifying, classifying, summarizing, inferring, comparing, and explaining beg for dialogue and interaction. There are a number of technological means for facilitating this type of collaboration through Web authoring: Weblogs, wikis, and Google Sites. These three tools enable groups of students to work collaboratively on writing and publishing content for the Internet. Where Weblogs (or blogs) and wikis each have unique features, Google Sites is more or less a combination of the two. The beauty of blogs, wikis, and Google Sites is that they serve as an extension of the classroom space and capitalize on the recent popularity of social networking.

Blogs

Essential to the blogging practice is a student's ability to closely read, interpret, and respond to the work of others through online writing. The integration of

blogs into an educational setting enables students to use a familiar medium as a means for expanding their connection to the curriculum and the outdoor experience. In addition, the capacity for blogs to be made public without the need for substantial resources provides students with an accessible and economical public platform from which they can explore new ideas and debate existing ones.

Where blogging differs from wikis and Google Sites is in the process for developing and adding content. As you will read in the sections that follow, wikis and Google Sites are designed to have many authors working on the same site, and while this can be true with blogs, the process for developing and posting the content is different.

The most popular blogging sites among teachers are Edublogs (www .edublogs.org), 21Classes (www.21classes.com), Wordpress (www.wordpress .com), and Google's Blogger (www.blogger.com). All of these sites have free memberships, and some allow for the creation of teacher accounts with student sub-accounts. Blogs have several useful features, some of which are shared by wikis and Google Sites:

1. *Custom title and address.* One feature that will remain constant for blogs, wikis, and Google Sites is the ability to have a custom title, as well as to maintain multiple sites.

2. *Posts.* Posting is simply making a new entry onto the blog site. When using blogs with your students, it is advised that you create one blog for your class/project, and then solicit content from the students that they want to have posted on that blog. Many blogs are not set up to be authored by a group, whereas wikis and Google Sites are. Teachers can assign certain groups of students to be responsible for the creation of the blog content for a given time period. When the content is complete, the teacher can copy and paste the content into a new blog post using his/her account.

3. *Blog comments.* Blogs are set up to handle back-and-forth (threaded) conversation on the same page. The best option for filtering comments is to select the permission setting that requires all comments to be approved by you before they are published on the blog.

4. *Custom "gadgets."* Blogs provide a multitude of modules and gadgets to add to your blog page: search fields, a blog description, archives of all of the blog posts, calendars, photos, slide shows, maps, news feeds, and so on.

Blogging is a safe, fast, customizable, and engaging way for students to begin constructing meaning, interpreting, exemplifying, classifying, summarizing, inferring, comparing, and explaining.

Wikis

A wiki is an online tool designed to foster the development of collaborative Web content. Students can see their work in relation to the work of classmates and as a collaborative process; their efforts go beyond just completing a project to be turned in. To create a wiki, I would suggest the following three sites as a starting point: Wikidot (www.wikidot.com), PBworks (www.pbworks.com), and, the most popular choice, Wikispaces (www.wikispaces.com). Although every wiki site will have its own protocol and language for developing content, let's talk about what you can generally expect when you begin the process of collaborative Web authoring.

Once you have a wiki site established, you will need to invite your students to join in the fun! This invitation process could involve your students having an e-mail account, so it's very important to make your students' parents aware of what they are about to do and to be compliant with CIPA and COPPA. Many teachers who use wikis with students under the age of 13 develop teacher accounts, with sub-accounts that do not require personal information for each student.

A certain amount of practice is needed to use wikis well. This is not to say that wikis are hard to use—many elementary school classrooms use them on a daily basis—but wikis require a slight learning curve. It is because of this learning curve that I suggest using Google Sites as an option for collaborative Web authoring.

Google Sites

Google Sites is a part of the larger suite of applications known as Google Apps. As with the wiki services, you will need to join Google Sites by signing up for a Google Apps account (or a Google Apps for Education account). By joining Google Apps, you now have access to the full suite of applications, including Google Calendar, YouTube, Google Docs, and a host of other applications. Similar to the wiki, you will need to invite collaborators to work on your Google Site. These collaborators need to have a Google Apps account,

so again, it is recommended that you involve your students' parents throughout the entire process.

Google created the Google Apps Education Edition as a way for schools to implement the suite of applications school- and district-wide and to solve issues surrounding compliance with CIPA and COPPA. Google Apps Education Edition includes the same applications as standard Google Apps; the applications can be mixed and matched depending on the needs of the school or district. Applications and implementation plans for Google Apps Education Edition can be found at www.google.com/educators/p_apps.html.

Outdoor Learning Application: Community Web Sites

The searching, bookmarking, note-taking progression has set up the fourth graders well for participating in a collaborative Web site. Working individually or in teams, students could begin to develop the pages they will need to display their emerging understanding of the content. As students continue to refine their online content, this is a great time to have students/teams invite a content expert to visit their pages and provide feedback.

Perhaps your curriculum lends itself to collecting data from your schoolyard and comparing it with other schoolyards. For example, let's say your class decided to look at the differences in bird alert distance (the distance between a human and a bird at the moment when a bird is alerted to the human's presence) when looking at birds in rural, suburban, and urban settings. Your students conducted extensive research on the type of birds that would be most common in all three locations, developed a research protocol for how to set up the feeder station to attract birds and measure the alert distance, and created a template for other schools to use to collect their own data. Using blogs, wikis, or Google Sites, students could develop a comprehensive page that provided would-be participants with all of the background and downloadable materials necessary to participate in the study.

The use of collaborative Web authoring can quickly evolve into a digital portfolio of your students' engagement with the outdoor learning experience. Students will have a record of the work they have done and how that work is connected to larger concepts and to the work of their peers. The public nature of the work will raise the level of concern students have for it and reinforces the authentic nature of outdoor learning. Learning in an outdoor setting is not done just for a grade, but as a way for students to connect with the world around them in meaningful and enriching ways.

Synchronous Collaborative Writing and Mind Mapping

Digital formats provide an excellent sandbox for collaborative thinking and writing. In the past, collaborative digital work usually entailed students e-mailing documents back and forth to one another or sharing a computer to work on the same project. Cloud computing has radically changed the collaborative process. Programs such as Google Docs (word processing/presentations/spreadsheets) and MindMeister (mind mapping) allow students to collaborate from across the room or across the globe—simultaneously! Cloud-based programs like these allow students to work on the same document at the same time because each document is stored in a central location on the Web, as opposed to documents stored on individual computers. These synchronous collaborative tools use color-coded text and name labels so students can see their own work as well as the work others are contributing in real time. The Google Docs suite of tools provides opportunities for students to collaborate on word-processing documents, multimedia presentations, and spreadsheet data collection and analysis. Sites such as TypeWith.me (http://typewith.me) and PrimaryPad (http://primarypad.com) provide the same synchronous writing experience without the need for an account. MindMeister (www.mindmeister.com) and Bubbl.us (https://bubbl.us/) provide a more visual approach to collaboration through their mind-mapping or concept-mapping tools. Concept mapping and mind mapping have long been lauded as exceptional ways to invite students to construct meaning, interpret, exemplify, classify, summarize, infer, compare, and explain, and synchronous collaborative mind mapping takes this process to another level. As an exercise in preparing for an outdoor learning experience, this process brings together multiple learning modalities and engages students kinesthetically, allowing them to move, shape, and build their ideas together.

Outdoor Learning Application: Collaborative Writing

Synchronous collaborative writing and mind mapping provides students with an engaging and collaborative space to construct meaning, interpret, exemplify, classify, summarize, infer, compare, and explain. One of the best uses I have seen for the integration of both these tools was with a teacher preparing his sixth-grade students for a schoolyard field trip to explore the runoff issues presented by a culvert on the school grounds. In this class, Google Docs was used to create a digital KWL chart (know/want to know/learned) as it related to their runoff research. Instead of just using their own school grounds as a focus, the students in this class made connections with three other sixth-grade classrooms across the school district.

Prior to starting their research, all four sixth-grade classes collaboratively developed the K (know) and W (want to know) sections. Students were able to see in real time the contributions each class was making. To conduct the runoff exploration, student teams were created using one student from each school. Each team had a collaborative mind map that they used to classify the research they had compiled. The culminating project involved each student team presenting their findings to all four classes simultaneously through the presentation function in Google Docs. Additional audio and video feeds were made possible through the use of Skype (also free) in all four classrooms.

Phase II: Midexperience

In Phase II, midexperience, practitioners need to provide students with structures and tools that will support engaged student participation. Technologically speaking, Phase II will be significantly different than Phase I for a number of reasons:

- Students are outside and involved in the learning experience itself. During this time, students need to be "unplugged" to allow their senses time to adapt to a new pace and place.

- The technology will probably be used periodically or as a supplement to careful observation and immersion in the outdoor classroom. Sending students out immediately with new technology such as cameras and GPS machines could detract from their initial experience.
- Technology will serve as a way to preserve the outdoor experience, giving students a way to capture the world around them and bring it back to the classroom for further study/inspiration.

Where Phase I focused on applications, Phase II will focus more on tools or peripherals that can help students apply, during the experience, what they learned in preparing for the experience. Before I describe the tools that will support this phase, let's look at how these tools should be introduced and used in an outdoor learning experience:

- *Take the time to introduce the tools.* Although using a digital camera may seem like a fairly common skill, some students need help. I have seen some excellent examples of teachers empowering students to create tutorials to teach their classmates how to use each of the new pieces of equipment.
- *Leave the technology inside during the first visits to the outdoor classroom.* The change in setting will be enough to process without the added distraction of monitoring and using tools. This ensures that a student's first interactions with nature outside are not through a viewfinder. A wonderful best practice for introducing these tools into the experience is to have students bring a log or a journal in which they will record the different features they would like to photograph, video record, audio record, and so on.
- *Develop a rotation or timing structure that will ensure that all students get to use the technology.* Connection with the natural world is personal. Make sure that all students share the tasks and have an opportunity to "see" the world.

Tools and Applications

The technology discussed in this section was selected based on what teachers have found to be the most effective at capturing or facilitating the outdoor learning experience, the least distracting to the outdoor experience, and the most user friendly for students of all ages. There are several types of technological gear that lend themselves well to outdoor learning:

- Digital photography and video
- Photo sharing
- Digital audio recording
- iPod Touch, iPad, and other tablet devices
- Global positioning systems (GPS)

Digital Photography and Video

A digital camera is one of the simplest, yet most effective, tools you can use to enhance your outdoor learning experiences. Cameras provide a cheap and easy way to collect data (using both still photos and video) or capture a moment that might otherwise be lost. When looking to purchase a class camera, or even a class set of cameras, the number one deciding factor will probably be cost. Chances are you will not have a lot of money to spend, so it will be a matter of finding the best camera for the best price. There are many features that companies tout about their products that are important, but not critical in your decision making. Take, for instance, camera resolution. Today, any digital camera you find on the market will have a resolution that will be more than sufficient for classroom use. If you were looking to create mass print publications or giant billboards, you might need to consider a high-resolution camera, but chances are you won't need it.

So what *is* important? When thinking about a classroom purchase, you must consider that your students will be the primary users of the tool. With this in mind, durability, easy-to-navigate menus, easy transfer of files, and standard battery sizes are at the top of the list. Judge durability by picking up the cameras and seeing how substantial they feel. Are they mostly plastic, or are the housings metal? Is the camera too big for little hands, or too heavy? These factors can lead to cameras being dropped more frequently. Next, navigate through the menus on the camera. At some point, you will need to change a setting or will need to show the students how to change a setting, and you want this to be relatively simple. As for file transfer, look to see whether the camera requires any special software to move images around. These additional programs can become a hassle and require more training to use.

Finally, batteries are a huge concern. Many cameras will use special proprietary batteries that are expensive to replace or to purchase. I always recommend cameras that take AAA or AA batteries simply because these batteries are accessible, and rechargeable versions of them are much cheaper than camera-specific batteries. The more spare batteries you have, the more your camera will stay in use.

Photo Sharing

You have a set of cameras poised and ready for your students to use. Kids have been properly trained, you have a rotation plan designed so all of the students will get a chance to use the equipment, and you have spent some time outside without the technology. You are ready! Fast-forward three days, and you are swimming in dozens of pictures that are unorganized, on five different computers, and not user friendly for the students. Help!

Flickr.com and Google's Picasa Web Albums are cloud-based services that provide users with a central location to store, organize, and share digital images. These services are also a gateway for finding other images posted by the millions of users with accounts.

Subscribing to these services is similar to the process of subscribing to any of the other Web-based services I have discussed (Picassa Web Albums is owned by Google, so if you have a Google account you are ready to roll), but in this case it is advisable to create and maintain only one account for the group. This eliminates the potential for unauthorized images to be posted. Students will still have access to their images, but not the permissions needed to add content to the site. In both services, students can easily search the site to find the images they took or find tagged images that deal with a specific outdoor experience.

Outdoor Learning Application: Photo Sharing

With most technologies in Phase II, it is difficult to explain how you could use them without having an understanding of the scope and sequence of the particular curriculum you are trying to teach in an outdoor setting. The most important part of Phase II is preparing the students to use the technology in a way that does not detract from the experience. Over the years, I have encountered a number of applications of digital photography that enhanced the outdoor learning process:

- Images of plants/gardens/spaces over time (time-lapse) and through the seasons

- A search for patterns on the school grounds (from simple to abstract)
- Human–environment interactions in the schoolyard (positive and negative)
- A visual land-use survey of how the schoolyard is used throughout the day and week
- Images from the schoolyard to use as story starters

Digital Audio Recording

Sometimes the best data collected from an outdoor learning experience are simply the sounds. Whether students are trying to capture the sounds of the environment around them, or their thoughts and reactions to the experience, audio data are powerful. Luckily, gathering this kind of data can be inexpensive, and editing the data is free.

A digital voice recorder (DVR) is the best choice for gathering audio data outside. This is due in part to the relatively low cost, portability, and ability to transfer data quickly from device to computer. In the $25 to $75 price range, you can obtain a DVR that will be more than suitable for data collection. Even within this price range, you will have a number of features to choose from:

- *Recording time versus quality.* When talking with teachers about their DVR purchases, many admitted to being swayed by the lure of longer recording times (some DVRs offer up to 250 hours). One teacher recounted the wisdom of her students when she was introducing the recorder to them. She boasted about the 100-plus hours of recording time for each of the ten DVRs, to which the students responded, "Why would we want to talk for that long? That's like, four days of talking—nonstop!" The most popular models for classroom use had only one to two and a half hours of recording time, but they had at least three levels of recording quality.
- *Recording and playback features:*

    Voice activation. This feature causes a device to automatically stop recording when it senses a silence, and to start recording when sound is heard again. This automatic feature is useful when students forget to start and stop recording. Voice activation can be troublesome because it might not register some sounds, such as birdcalls or wind, as worthy to record. Make sure your DVR allows you to turn voice activation on and off, or has a sensitivity setting that will go low enough to be triggered by ambient sounds.

Recording folders. Many DVRs allow you to establish a series of folders to sort your audio on the machine itself. This can be helpful when using the machines with multiple classes.

Automatic power shutdown. Regardless of whether the DVR runs on an internal rechargeable battery or replaceable AAA batteries, this simple feature will save you frustration, time, and money.

- *Data transfer.* When purchasing a DVR, look for "PC connectivity." PC connectivity means that it will work with a PC, but not necessarily with a Mac. You will need to look for the Mac compatible logo on the box to make sure it will work with a Mac. USB is the primary means for transferring your content from the DVR to the computer. DVRs that record using WMA and/or MP3 audio formats have some of the easiest transfer processes. While USB data transfer is the fastest and easiest way to move audio from the device to the computer, some of the cheapest models will not have this as an option. By connecting an audio cable to the microphone jack of your DVR to your computer, you can record the audio content on the computer as it is played from the DVR. To record the audio coming from the DVR, you will need to use an audio recording application on the computer. A favorite application among teachers is called Audacity, which is a free download from http://audacity.sourceforge.net (both PC and Mac versions are available). This program allows you to record audio coming into your computer and save it in a variety of formats. Beyond just recording, Audacity also allows you to crop audio and mix audio files together, making this program a must. Another popular audio editing program for Mac users is GarageBand (preloaded on Mac computers as a part of their iLife suite).

Outdoor Learning Application: Audio Recording

Audio recording is a simple, yet effective, tool for connecting with the outdoor environment. One of the most interesting applications of this methodology was illustrated with an integrated middle school language arts class. The teacher had developed a yearlong exploration that integrated creative writing with the study of seasonal change. Throughout the year, students developed a range of creative pieces related to the passing seasons. Students performed their pieces outside and recorded themselves, paying particular attention to the changes in sounds the outdoor environment would bring during each season. Some students chose to integrate just the sounds they recorded each season as a soundtrack for their written/spoken words. Throughout the experience, students talked about how the outdoor environment truly became a character in their work, which inspired them to find new and meaningful ways to weave it into future works.

iPod Touch, iPad, and Other Tablet Devices

Before discussing global positioning systems, I would be remiss if I did not describe the rise of tablet options as a means for enhancing outdoor learning. Currently, the iPod Touch, by Apple, is a small, handheld, touch-operated device that contains all of the photo and audio collection capabilities discussed previously, but in one device. In addition, it also has the capability to record video and, with supplemental software, the ability to edit the video, photos, and audio into a complete movie. The computing power in such a small device is staggering and provides a realistic all-in-one option for teachers. While the iPods may record audio, video, and photos at a lower quality, for a majority of classroom applications, it will work exceptionally well. In addition, the added features, such as the ability to access the Internet and download and use hundreds of thousands of applications through the iTunes App Store, makes this device a handheld computer, not just an imaging tool.

Apple also offers a larger device, the iPad (9.7-inch display size), that has many of the same functions as the iPod Touch, but with a larger screen. The iPad is in the leading wave of a new resurgence of tablet computing. The tech world seems to have found a good mix between size and function. As learning tools, these devices will only continue to evolve and provide new and exciting modes to enhance both indoor and outdoor learning environments.

Global Positioning Systems

Global positioning system (GPS) technology has exploded in the past few years, making it possible to find inexpensive GPS machines as well as the integration of GPS into a host of devices, including cell phones and digital cameras (not in the iPod Touch yet, but it is present in the more advanced iPad with 3G connectivity). As a classroom tool and outdoor enhancement, the GPS has a wonderful niche. Where cameras and camcorders show you what your surroundings look like, the GPS actually tells students where they are in the world. This type of location data can be used in many ways in the classroom.

When selecting a GPS device for classroom use, it is most important to remember that the "in-car" units we hear so much about come loaded with a host of maps and other information that are useful when driving down an unfamiliar section of highway—not your schoolyard. In an outdoor classroom setting, teachers have found the basic, handheld, nonmapping models to be the most user friendly and beneficial to student engagement. Keep in mind that a nonmapping GPS can record location data and tell you how to return to a certain location.

Simplicity is key for a GPS for classroom use. A basic GPS device starts at around $100, with features that will work beautifully in a classroom setting. More expensive features, such as additional memory, color screens, touch screens, and mapping (to give you turn-by-turn directions), are not critical. Some GPS devices will allow you to upload additional maps, such as topographic maps, but you will need to decide whether this is worth the additional cost.

In the past, special software was required to work with the data recorded on GPS machines. With the addition of Google Earth and its close integration with GPS data, this information can be plotted quickly. Google Earth can import the tracks, waypoints, and routes recorded by the GPS—even the simplest ones. In a classroom setting, tracks, waypoints, and routes will be your primary sources of data, and the ease of integration with Google Earth will help make this data come alive.

Outdoor Learning Application: GPS

The GPS device offers a unique spatial awareness perspective on outdoor learning. Students make connections to their surroundings and unwrap abstract concepts such as distance and space. It is one thing to read that an object is 200 yards away, and it is another to actually go out and pace off the same distance. North, south, east, and west move from just directional language to associated landmarks on the school grounds.

As a spatial device, the GPS has numerous mapping connections. With the integration of Google Earth, students can bring location data back into the classroom and see it in relation to the wider school grounds, city, state, and beyond. A particularly interesting application of GPS in an outdoor learning experience was when fifth-grade students used their GPS machines to mark the locations of their outdoor reading "sit-spots" during language arts. After recording their locations, students traded their GPS devices. Students followed the GPS information on their classmates' devices to introduce one another to their respective sit-spot locations. The same class of fifth graders also signed out the GPS devices so they could mark the locations of nonnative species throughout their community after school hours. They uploaded their GPS data and digital images they'd also taken to make a class multimedia map that was presented to local environmental agencies.

One of the great resources for GPS activities is the USGS Education page for GPS, maps, and compasses (http://education.usgs.gov/common/lessons/gps.html). Here you will find links to a number of useful GPS resources, including classroom ideas, technical information, and advanced GPS usage. Another GPS favorite among classroom teachers is geocaching. A comprehensive Web site for this activity is found at www.geocaching.com. The site describes the activity:

> *Geocaching is a high-tech treasure hunting game played throughout the world by adventure seekers equipped with GPS devices. The basic idea is to locate hidden containers, called geocaches,*

outdoors and then share your experiences online. Geocaching is enjoyed by people from all age groups, with a strong sense of community and support for the environment. (2011)

Many teachers have created private caches for their classes and schools that provide the same level of excitement that a cache in another town could create. Private caches are a wonderful way to feature the various aspects of the schoolyard. Students who have further interest can find close to 850,000 caches all across the globe through the Geocaching.com site.

While it may be somewhat limited in its scope, GPS drawing, or GPS art, is another unique integration of spatial technology and the arts. This concept is exactly as it sounds—drawing with a GPS device. Essentially, everywhere you move, the GPS will trace your movements. If you try hard enough, you can coordinate your movements in such as way as to "draw." There are some humorous spoofs of this on the Internet, but the actual products represent some complex and thoughtful work.

Phase III: Postexperience

In Phase III, postexperience, teachers should provide students with opportunities to reflect on, synthesize, and evaluate conclusions that have emerged from their outdoor experiences.

Tools and Applications

It is important that students are engaged with meaningful and engaging outcomes and are provided with supportive technologies that will enhance their abilities to analyze, evaluate, and create. The technologies featured in this section are just the beginning of what exists. These tools were chosen because of their popularity with teachers and their ability to engage students in both independent and collaborative analysis, evaluation, and creation.

Collaborative Writing/Presentation Tools

MindMeister was presented as a mind-mapping tool in the section on Phase I, but depending on your desired outcomes, a tool such as this could be useful for Phase III as well. If you would like your students to do more collaborative writing as opposed to mapping, applications such as Zoho Writer (http://writer.zoho.com) and Writeboard (http://writeboard.com) offer options for group writing. But what if you are interested in an application that will work on both individual and collaborative levels—an application that will give you an opportunity to view, edit, and provide feedback to your students across a range of document types? To cover all of these bases, Google Docs is still your best bet.

With Google Docs, students can choose to create a document (word processing), spreadsheet, or presentation (multimedia slide presentation). As with Google Sites, all three of these products can be created in a collaborative, synchronous manner. What teachers find most exciting about using Google Docs as a collaborative writing and presentation tool are the ways in which their students connect and integrate the various modes of technological inquiry. For example, separate applications such as Google Sites, Google Earth, and Google Docs can be woven together as an expression of individual and collective analysis, evaluation, and creation. Students can move from a spatial analysis in Google Earth to a collaborative analysis of their findings in a Google Document, and finally present their work to the world via a Google Site. What makes this process even more exciting is that it can be done in collaboration with other students across the world. In this setting, cooperative learning and collaboration are not limited to those in the classroom, in fact, the world becomes the classroom. To access Google Docs, follow the same exact process used to access Google Sites.

Podcasts

Podcasting is a way for students to express new ideas and understanding through a produced audio transmission. Students are the writers, producers, directors, and actors in their own audio productions. These productions can take on many forms, from creative fictional audio dramas to research-supported, nonfiction audio documentaries. The genre of your podcasts will be influenced by the objectives your students are working toward.

When looking to use podcasting, I suggest that you go through the process of making one as a whole class before you send your students off to create their own. The most successful teachers also use storyboarding and scripting sessions as a way to help organize and plan their podcasts.

Podcasts are to be listened to, not stored on a computer with no audience, but how can you get your students' podcasts heard by others? One option is to make your class podcasts available through iTunes (www.apple.com/itunes/podcasts/specs.html). The one issue with hosting through a service such as iTunes is the expectation that new podcasts will be coming on a regular basis. If your students are not creating an ongoing series of podcasts, then the better option is to host the podcasts on your own class/project Web site. Teachers like this option for several reasons:

- The podcast is viewed in context with the other work that the students have completed.
- Access for parents and community members is easy.
- The students have a greater sense of ownership and pride when their work is hosted on their site. I cannot tell you how many teachers have said this. One teacher recounted the story of when he excitedly told his students he had figured out how to get their work linked to iTunes, to which the students replied, "Why would we want it there? We have our own site!"

Teachers who choose to host podcasts on their own sites should get the word out! Chances are people won't be looking for the class's podcasts, but if you create and send some focused e-mail invitations to those who may have an interest, or use other social media outlets such as Facebook and Twitter to generate "buzz," traffic to the project will greatly increase.

Digital Stories and Podumentaries

These two strategies are discussed together because they are similar in intent; however, they use slightly different technologies. Digital storytelling is a technological expansion on the art of storytelling. In this modernized version, students weave together digital images, video, music, narrative, and voice to convey meaning and to tell the story of people, places, and events. Digital stories differ from podcasting in that they add the element of visual imagery.

Podumentaries, on the other hand, are short, nonfiction digital videos that explore student-selected or assigned topics. While they still emphasize the collaborative processes and participatory production of digital stories, they are not focused on first-person narratives—the topics are wide open.

Both of these options are a great venue for all of the digital images, videos, and audio recordings collected throughout outdoor learning experiences. Depending on the focus of your experience, digital stories or podumentaries could provide a powerful platform for both individual and collaborative creation.

In a print book, it is difficult to provide examples for these two strategies because they are multimedia-intensive, but a great place to start is at the Center for Digital Storytelling (www.storycenter.org). Also available through The Center for Digital Storytelling is the *Digital Storytelling Cookbook* (www .storycenter.org/cookbook.html). This is a fantastic manual that provides extensive guidance for creating digital stories, but the elements described work wonderfully for developing podumentaries as well.

iMovie (for Mac) and Windows Movie Maker (for PC) are excellent free options for creating both digital stories and podumentaries, but both types of projects could also be created using a presentation software program such as PowerPoint. These programs can mix together digital images, music, narrative, voice, and, in a limited way, video. In using presentation software, you will sacrifice the complexity and control of titles, transitions, and timings, but it is a familiar and easy program to start with that allows students to think in "frames" as opposed to the linear production that the movie programs require.

Teachers who have created both digital stories and podumentaries find presentation software adequate, but far too cumbersome for more advanced video usage. Eventually, they transition their students to iMovie and Windows Movie Maker.

As with podcasting, students and teachers need to be aware of fair use when using copyrighted material. iMovie provides access to the same non-copyrighted music and sound effects that are available in GarageBand, and you might also try Creative Commons (http://creativecommons.org) if your program does not provide these features.

Sharing Students' Work

Let's talk distribution. Once students have created masterful works, how can the works be seen? If you have developed a class/project Web site, you should be able to embed all of the media your students have created through YouTube or through direct upload to your site. As discussed with podcasts, I suggest that you target specific populations, such as same grade levels in other district buildings, to alert them to the presence of your students' new Web content. It is always a thrill to have others enjoy your students' work, but sometimes students will have to wait for a long time for someone to find their work if an invitation is not supplied.

While the Web is a great way for students to share work, many teachers have found hosting a "world premiere" at the school or local library is an empowering way for showcasing student work. While posting to the Internet does open the work up to a large audience, the thrill students gain from introducing their work to an audience in person and seeing it enjoyed is priceless.

Conclusion

The integration of Web 2.0, cloud-based, and audio, image, and sound technologies into a phased approach for outdoor learning can have a profound effect on the students involved. When used in a phased approach, the students will experience a progression of using technologies that enhance their outdoor learning experience.

In Phase I, preexperience, the strategic application of technology can help enhance the students' ability to build foundational knowledge, develop initial interpretations, express and research concerns, and seek clarity about expectations. In Phase II, midexperience, technological means can be helpful in developing a chronological diary for any given experience and can provide auditory and visual cues for future analysis, evaluation, and reflection. This archive can serve as a critical tool for understanding the changes and learning that occurred throughout the experience. And finally, in Phase III, postexperience, technology can help enhance the outdoor experience through novel and innovative opportunities to reflect on, synthesize, and evaluate conclusions; engage in dialogue with others regarding their personal and collective growth; and create new works that express their understanding.

Thoughtful and well-planned integration of technology will help to ease the tension between the natural world and the electronic world. The natural world needs to be experienced, but there are a lot of ways technology can facilitate long-lasting effects from those experiences and help students to see their connection to the natural world in both deeper and broader contexts.

Roberta Paolo, also known
as Granny

Spotlight 5
Granny's Garden School

When I first heard about Granny's Garden School (www.grannysgardenschool.com), I had to chuckle at the name. Little did I know that Granny's is considered by many to be the largest and most comprehensive school garden program in the Midwest. And, there really is a Granny! An absolutely amazing Granny who in less than four years was able to create one of the most unique school and community outdoor learning partnerships that I have ever seen.

"Gardens Are About Picking and Sharing"

Roberta Paolo has always loved gardening. She also is convinced that gardens are good for children. Her two grandchildren were frequent visitors to her home and helped her tend the flower beds that often yielded surplus plants. She ran ads in the free section of the local paper offering to give away the extras. Many new gardeners responded, and she often spent time sharing gardening tips with her new friends.

Roberta feels strongly that gardens are about picking and sharing, not just for looking and admiring. If people stopped to look at her gardens she would pick them a bouquet, and children were always invited to pick a flower to take home. She tells the wonderful story of the day when a small group of teenage "tough guys" happened to congregate near her yard and began talking loudly and inappropriately. She approached the group and explained that her grandchildren

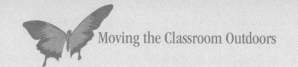

were outside and she would rather that they didn't hear that type of language. Since she happened to have some flowers in her hand, she spontaneously gave each one a bloom as she talked. Roberta says that she truly saw the "power of the flower" when the tough exteriors melted away and the tough guys were momentarily again little boys politely saying, "I'll take this home to my Mom."

During the fall of 2001, Roberta was picking up her grandchildren at the primary school in Loveland, Ohio, when she noticed a lady planting mums in front of the building. As Roberta says, "A light went on in my head! Wow! Look at the possibilities here. It had never occurred to me that one could plant something at school." After talking with school administrators and getting school board approval, Roberta launched her plan to create a garden bed at the school the following spring. Her mission was clear and tangible: Roberta simply wanted to give kids a chance to pick flowers. She developed garden activities, and a few teachers signed up to participate in the planting. By the fall, there were seventeen teachers wanting their own class gardens. Currently, fifty-five classroom gardens are being used to teach content across the curriculum.

A Garden Becomes a Program

What has transpired in the seven years since the first garden was planted is both inspiring and spectacular. Not only are there classroom garden beds, but common garden areas have been created literally on every square foot of perimeter around the two buildings on the site. A 7-acre nature trail has also been created on the complex, and several outdoor learning areas with student seating dot the 25-acre campus.

Common garden areas like this create learning spaces that are both beautiful and functional.

Volunteers have been an important part of the success. Eagle Scout efforts have added over a dozen projects to the site. Scouts have constructed five outdoor classroom areas, a bridge on the nature trail, a bird blind, an arbor, herb gardens, fences, numerous garden boxes, and a three-section composter. Granny even has a list of suggested future scout projects on her Web site.

By the end of three years, Roberta's initial idea of a garden where children could pick flowers had blossomed (pardon the pun) into an entire program, not just a flower bed. But it was getting increasingly difficult for one person to provide support for teachers interested in using the gardens while managing and scheduling the steady stream of volunteers needed to maintain acres of garden space. As the number of garden areas grew, the weeding and watering of plantings became a problem. Especially during the summer, Roberta found that sign-up sheets and volunteer scheduling just didn't work reliably. As her program expanded, she also investigated other school garden programs around the country. She frequently heard the sad but all-too-familiar scenario of excellent projects falling into disuse and neglect when the originator was no longer involved.

Roberta was very concerned that her program have the help it needed, as well as stability and longevity. The solution was simple, yet bold. In 2006 she formed a nonprofit corporation called Granny's Garden School, Inc. The corporation is governed by a seven-member board of directors, with Roberta serving as the executive direc-

tor. By establishing a nonprofit corporation, Roberta not only provided long-term continuity for her program but also made it possible for individuals and businesses to make charitable contributions to underwrite expenses. It was now possible to pay people to help with garden maintenance, classroom programs, and the development of special events. Granny's Garden School now has six part-time employees, three of whom work primarily with classroom teachers to facilitate lessons in the gardens that correlate with the curriculum.

Classroom planting beds help to enhance the curriculum.

The following is the mission of Granny's Garden School:

> Granny's Garden School uses public school grounds to help students experience nature, the satisfaction of growing their own food and to appreciate the simple pleasure of picking a flower. We collaborate with schools to offer hands-on learning opportunities that complement the school's curriculum. (Granny's Garden School 2010a)

Promoting the Program and Securing Resources

A quick look at Granny's Garden School Web site verifies that Roberta is a natural when it comes to sales and marketing. Since the school garden program receives no direct financial support from the school district, all the money and materials needed to support this complex operation

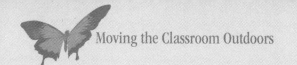
have to be generated through donations to the nonprofit corporation. But Roberta doesn't just focus on fund-raising; she also provides activities for "friend-raising." The fund-raising efforts include a plant sale in May and a mum sale in September. In addition, Granny's Garden School sponsors a Pick-a-Bouquet Club. For a suggested donation of $35, you join the club and may pick ten bouquets of up to twenty-four stems each from Granny's Gardens. The program is available from June through October and includes flowers and herbs. (Granny emphasizes that the picking of flowers has to be done outside of school hours.)

"Friend-raising" efforts include a Grandparent's Day in the gardens, tasting parties, and a Harvest Celebration. Held in September, the Harvest Celebration features an eclectic mix of activities, food, gardening-related information, and just plain fun in the outdoors.

A major source of assistance comes from commercial and community supporters, who are listed on the Garden School Web site. Granny even includes hyperlinks to the Web sites of businesses. She regularly sends bouquets from the gardens to businesses that have provided volunteers to help at the school site.

During the summer, Granny's Garden School also sponsors the Teaching in the Garden Camp for School Garden Developers. "The week-long camp focuses on low-cost methods for establishing a school garden program and how to integrate the garden with classroom curriculum" (Granny's Garden School 2010b). This excellent professional development opportunity provides information about both best gardening practices and best outdoor learning practices. Participants spend the week in one of the most extensive living displays of school gardening options I have ever seen. Practical hands-on activities help potential school garden developers explore what they may be able to incorporate on their own school sites.

Although not a way to raise funds, but rather to provide cheer in the community, Granny instituted the Bouquets on Wheels program. This has to be one of the most beautiful examples of community outreach that I have seen in an outdoor education program. Classrooms carefully prepare fifty mini-bouquets from flowers that they have picked from their school gardens, with the blooms inserted in florist water tubes. Students also write short notes or make drawings to accompany the bouquets. The bouquets are then given to the local Meals on Wheels organization and provide a touch of unexpected beauty as they are distributed along with lunch to area senior citizens. Children not only feel connected to the garden but also experience the satisfaction of sharing beauty with others. Such a simple idea, but what a powerful activity!

A Unique Concept and an Amazing Lady

Granny's Garden School is truly an amazing enterprise. It has provided Loveland Primary and Elementary Schools with a resource that would simply be impossible for a school to duplicate.

Nearly every child who attends these schools is provided with an opportunity to learn about nature on a school site that is filled with beauty as well as meaningful site enhancements.

I have never seen anything quite like Granny's Garden School. The concept of forming a nonprofit to provide outdoor education to one public school campus is truly unique, and certainly does provide a way to secure the resources needed to carry out an ongoing program.

But this story is not just about nonprofits or clever fund-raising. This is about an amazing lady who wanted to share her love of gardening and flowers with children. She has even moved to a home that adjoins the school grounds so that she can be near her gardens. Her modest house is almost entirely engulfed by Granny's Garden School. There are bulb and seed storage rooms, sorting and packaging rooms, a meeting room for the board of directors, and a backyard filled with plantings that are being started for later inclusion in the school gardens. As Roberta says, she is not a person who separates her personal life from her work. Gardening is her life and her passion. The Loveland community is indeed fortunate to have her in its midst.

Chapter 6
A Little More Information

In earlier chapters I mentioned several organizations that may not be familiar to readers. In this chapter I have tried to provide a brief overview of the benefits each group offers to schoolyard planners. Take a look at the Web sites and you will find an abundance of resources and more descriptive detail about each organization.

Also included in this chapter is contact information for selected schools. In researching material for this book, I traveled to twenty-three schools in eight states. Every school visit added unique ideas and practicality to these pages. Although every school site had interesting and useful enhancements, it would be very wordy and not especially helpful to describe each one in detail. Instead, I highlight and provide contact information for a few representative schools with unique features.

Organizations

It would be impossible to list, or even count, all of the local, state, and national organizations that have information, materials, and expertise to contribute to schoolyard planners. As I contacted schools, however, I heard several orga-

nizations mentioned frequently. Please understand that this is certainly not a comprehensive list of helpful organizations, nor are the groups listed here the only providers of information on specific topics. Use this section as a starting point for beginning your exploration of available resources.

The Fruit Tree Planting Foundation

According to the Web site of the Fruit Tree Planting Foundation (www.ftpf.org), this unique organization is dedicated to "planting fruitful trees and plants to alleviate world hunger, combat global warming, strengthen communities, and improve the surrounding air, soil, and water" (2005a). The foundation awards grants to nonprofits, public schools, and government entities that own the planting sites and can ensure long-term commitment to care for the plantings.

For schools, the foundation has created a "Fruit Tree 101" program that creates "outdoor edible classrooms, where students meet to learn about botany, ecology, and how to protect the planet's health" (Fruit Tree Planting Foundation 2005b). There is a planting weekend using local volunteers, which takes place under the supervision of a certified arborist provided by the foundation. There also is a session for students led by foundation instructors that emphasizes the importance of trees for the environment and fruit in the diet, and culminates in a group tree-planting exercise.

The Fruit Tree 101 application form is not complex and centers around the practical and logistical concerns that are involved with planting a number of trees and shrubs on a site. By applying, the school ensures the future care and maintenance of the plantings. All trees do not have to be placed in the same area like a typical orchard, but can be scattered throughout the school site. Schools usually need to have space to accommodate twenty to twenty-five trees planted at 15-foot intervals. This is a great way to get trees and shrubs for your school site, as well as technical expertise about planting.

Earth Partnership for Schools

As I researched exemplary school sites to visit for this book, I soon found that several schools had participated in the Earth Partnership for Schools (EPS) program (http://uwarboretum.org/eps). I had the opportunity to meet with Cheryl Bauer-Armstrong, director of EPS, and learn firsthand about this program that is having a profound impact on both teachers and students.

According to the facilitator handbook, EPS started in 1991 "as an outgrowth of the University of Wisconsin Arboretum's focus on ecological restoration as a way of establishing a positive relationship between people and the land" (University of Wisconsin Arboretum 2009).

The cornerstone of EPS is a two-week summer institute that brings together teams of teachers, resource personnel, and community members. Ideally, teams represent individual school buildings. The institute focuses on a variety of outcomes: emphasizing historical and technical knowledge about native garden sites, and focusing on instructional methods, assessment issues, and collaborative strategies for implementing a restoration-based curriculum on a school site.

Earth Partnership for Schools places a strong emphasis on the use of the school site as an instructional tool. The development and utilization of native garden sites serves as the major organizer for the program. An extensive K–12 Curriculum Guide has been developed and includes nearly 100 carefully designed activities that relate beautifully to the restoration theme.

Based on the tremendous success of EPS in Wisconsin, the Restoration-Education, Science Training, and Outreach for Regional Educators (RESTORE) initiative was established to replicate the EPS program in other states. To date, EPS centers are located in fourteen states (CA, IL, IN, KS, KY, MD, MI, MN, MO, NC, NH, OK, OR, WI) and Puerto Rico and provide adaptable environmental education models across the country for those who are interested in restoration ecology on schoolyards.

I have been amazed at the depth, commitment, technical quality, and educational best practices that are integral components of the EPS program. I would strongly encourage any school that has an emerging interest in schoolyard-enhanced learning to contact Earth Partnership for Schools and inquire about training programs. The national expansion provided by RESTORE may mean that there is a summer institute in your geographic region.

Environmental Concern, Inc.

Environmental Concern (www.wetland.org) is a nonprofit organization that is committed to working with all aspects of wetlands. The organization's education division "works to increase understanding of, foster appreciation for, and encourage the stewardships of wetland systems. This is accomplished through materials/curriculum development, schoolyard habitat development and innovative outreach programs" (Environmental Concern 2010).

I learned of Environmental Concern (EC) while visiting Park Forest Elementary in State College, Pennsylvania. Park Forest had received a grant through Environmental Concern and was in the midst of constructing a small wetland area (about 1,000 square feet) beside the school building. EC does not have grant funding available every year, but the organization is always able to provide valuable advice and resource information on the two most essential factors in school wetland construction—design and plant selection. Although we often think of a wetland as a large area, students can learn much from a carefully planned wetland that is only a few thousand square feet in size.

Initially, three teachers and the principal from Park Forest attended a planning workshop along with others in the region that had received grants. Soon after the workshop, a wetlands educator from EC traveled to Park Forest and helped the school evaluate sites for a future wetland. The EC educator then presented a possible design for the wetland, discussed a time line, and identified key decisions that would have to be made. Probably of most importance, the EC educator met with district physical plant staff to talk about digging on the site. The EC educator even helped with plant selection, and had students assist with deciding what plants would be best for the site. On planting day, the EC educator returned again with plants and tools to coordinate a celebration of wetlands day, which gave each of the 500 students in the building a chance to be a part of the planting process.

As a part of the Park Forest grant, a training workshop was provided by EC in its Wonders of Wetlands (WOW) curriculum. All teachers in the building could attend to learn how to bring wetlands into their curriculum and to experience techniques for taking students out to study in the new outdoor classroom.

Like the Fruit Tree Planting Foundation, Environmental Concern provides on-site help with key technical decisions that can make or break a schoolyard enhancement project. The presence of an outside expert can also add more credibility and energy to a project. By all means, explore what these two organizations might be able to offer to your school. Their Web sites have extensive resource materials that are valuable in their own right.

U.S. Fish and Wildlife Service Schoolyard Habitat Program

The U.S. Fish and Wildlife Service (USFWS) is doing wonderful things to promote the development and use of the schoolyard as a learning resource.

A few years ago USFWS developed the *Schoolyard Habitat Project Guide* (USFWS 2010) through its Chesapeake Bay Field Office. This 133-page guide carefully outlines the steps needed to create three types of habitats on a school site: forest, wetland, and meadow.

The guide begins with a general overview of the planning process and then outlines in detail how to develop each type of habitat. What makes this publication especially useful is that it approaches the development of each habitat from two perspectives. First, teachers are provided with background material and technical information regarding the habitat. Next, there are very specific activities to involve students in the project. Worksheets, data recording forms, and background information written especially for students are included. Materials in the guide were inspired by actual schoolyard improvement projects, and teachers and administrators served as close advisors to the project. The *Schoolyard Habitat Project Guide* definitely is worth a look—it is free to download (www.fws.gov/ChesapeakeBay/pdf/habitatguide.pdf), and many of the student activities could be used in a variety of content areas.

The USFWS has just completed a major revision of the habitat project guide. The revised version incorporates the best of the previous guide and is filled with practical examples of planning procedures and tips for implementation of a schoolyard habitat program. Since the guides are quite different in structure, I encourage you to look at both versions if possible. The newly revised guide is available at www.fws.gov/cno/conservation/schoolyard.cfm.

Another excellent resource available from the Chesapeake Bay site of the USFWS is the publication *Common Qualities of Excellent Schoolyard Habitats* (Maryland Schoolyard Habitat Partnership 2010). This is a crystallization of the primary purposes and general goals that should be a part of schoolyard habitat development programs. The publication makes a great discussion starter for parent and faculty groups that are exploring outdoor site enhancement.

Evergreen

Evergreen is a Canadian nonprofit organization that, since 1991, has worked to engage Canadians in "sustaining dynamic outdoor spaces—in schools, communities and homes" (Evergreen 2010).

School ground greening is one of Evergreen's major initiatives, delivered through its Toyota Evergreen Learning Grounds program. The Learning Grounds program brings school communities together to transform barren school grounds into healthy, natural, and creative outdoor classrooms. To achieve this,

Learning Grounds provides funding, expert assistance from a national network of professional greening associates, and an extensive publication library, available for download at their Web site (www.evergreen.ca). These resources provide information on everything from planning and design, to research, case studies, and maintenance, to their Native Plant Database from which schools can pick native and heritage plant species for planting.

The Evergreen site also includes many examples of schoolyard greening efforts throughout Canada. The organization serves as a clearinghouse for innovative ways to enhance instruction through outdoor learning. This site should definitely be on your "must-see" list if you are beginning to explore schoolyard-enhanced learning.

Children and Nature Network

According to its Web site, the Children and Nature Network (C&NN) "was created to encourage and support the people and organizations working nationally and internationally to reconnect children with nature. The network provides a critical link between researchers and individuals, and educators and organizations, dedicated to children's health and well-being" (Children and Nature Network 2010).

The organization takes much of its impetus from Richard Louv's (2005) influential book *Last Child in the Woods: Saving Our Children from Nature-Deficit Disorder*. The C&NN Web site has an extensive array of articles, links, video clips, and current news reports that relate to children and the outdoors.

A tremendously useful and unique feature of the site is its annotated bibliography of current research studies that focus on themes related to children and nature. The summaries are well organized, written in very understandable language, and contain complete bibliographic references. For many studies there are even links to the complete document. In our evidence-driven culture, it is often necessary to be able to cite research that supports outdoor learning activities. The C&NN site's "Research and Publications" tab can save hours of time for the teacher or administrator who is looking for documentation to present to an outdoor learning skeptic (Children and Nature Network 2011).

The National Wildlife Federation Schoolyard Habitat Program

The National Wildlife Federation (NWF) offers a variety of planning resources for schools interested in creating outdoor learning spaces. From their Schoolyard Habitats Web site (http://www.nwf.org/Get-Outside/Outdoor-Activities/Garden-for-Wildlife/Schoolyard-Habitats.aspx) you can access a "How-to Guide for Schoolyard Habitats" as well as a great selection of sample lesson plans. The Web site provides practical advice for schoolyard planners and has links to dozens of other agencies and resources.

It is also possible to have your schoolyard habitat certified as part of the NWF's Certified Wildlife Habitat program (http://www.nwf.org/Get-Outside/Outdoor-Activities/Garden-for-Wildlife/Schoolyard-Habitats/Certify-Your-Schoolyard.aspx). According to the NWF Web site, "Certifying your site will bring media attention and national recognition for your school community's hard work. Also, once you are certified, you can enjoy the Schoolyard Habitats listserv and quarterly newsletter, and be eligible to order a Schoolyard Habitats sign for your outdoor classroom. Certification brings your school into a dynamic network of certified schools, and gives you access to special resources and information from the National Wildlife Federation" (National Wildlife Federation 2011).

The NWF has produced high-quality educational materials for many years. By all means take a look at their helpful resources for enhancing your school site.

Global Gardens

Global Gardens defines itself as "a non-profit organization dedicated to empowering students and communities through hands-on science education. We believe helping students create a garden is a way to not only assist them in learning about science, health and the environment but also challenge them to become caring, forward thinking and confident individuals. Global Gardens is committed to planting seeds of change!" (Global Gardens 2010).

This unique organization based in Tulsa, Oklahoma, was established in 2007 and currently serves 1,100 students at two sites. It combines school-day gardening programs with an extensive after-school component. What is unique about the Global Gardens program is the intentional inclusion of peace education. The emphasis upon conflict resolution through peaceful mediation is beautifully evidenced by the peace tables that students designed for their garden spaces.

Accessible on the Web site are two excellent examples of effective communication about gardening projects. The *Global Gardens Times* is a newspaper

created by one after-school group and contains a delightful accumulation of recipes, games, gardening tips, creative writing, and artwork. The organization's blog (www.globalgardens.blogspot.com/), with its easily accessible archive, also includes a wide variety of entries about projects and activities that could easily spark adaptations at other schools.

Schools

Although each of the following schools has a wide variety of schoolyard enhancement and outdoor learning initiatives, I highlight only a few aspects that are unique to these sites. In most cases I include the Web site of the school district rather than of the individual building. It is helpful to get an overview of the school district first and then use the links to individual buildings that are found on the district home page.

Park Forest Elementary School

2181 School Drive
State College, PA 16803
814-231-5010
www.scasd.org
Contact person: Donnan Stoicovy, principal

Everyone agrees that professional development is essential for outdoor learning, but finding sustained, building-wide examples can be difficult. Park Forest is an excellent example of professional development that spans all grade levels and is viewed as a continuous process.

The school makes good use of collegial discussion teams. The teams use the general theme of schoolyard learning, but then refine a topic to meet the emerging interests of the team. Before beginning the discussion groups, all staff complete an extensive survey to assess the level of acceptance of outdoor learning as well as the types of resources needed to use the schoolyard as an effective instructional tool. Collegial discussion groups meet throughout the school year to maintain interest and focus.

Park Forest also is a good example of a building that participates in a professional development school (PDS) model with a university. It is interesting to see the PDS model, with its emphasis on both theory and practice, being used to help a staff focus on outdoor learning.

Brookside Elementary

6700 McVey Boulevard
Columbus, OH 43235
614-883-2750
www.worthington.k12.oh.us
Contact person: Fritz Monroe, principal

Brookside is a good example of a school that has decided to center its emphasis on developing twenty-first-century skills around the concept of outdoor learning. After seeking community and staff input, the decision was made to emphasize the experiential hands-on focus that is integral to outdoor learning. Students use a variety of process skills by gathering and interpreting data from outdoor experiences. Technology also plays a key role as students gather, organize, analyze, and display data at Brookside.

Brookside has an eclectic mix of outdoor learning site enhancements. To carry out his goal of providing infrastructure for outdoor learning, Principal Fritz Monroe has coordinated, facilitated, and even personally constructed a variety of learning venues. The school site includes areas such as a tortoise enclosure in a courtyard, a butterfly garden, extensive raised planting beds, a retention pond with a study pier and outdoor seating area, an indoor bird blind looking out on a courtyard, and an orchard (provided through the Fruit Tree Planting Foundation). The school also is an excellent example of community involvement. The raised planting beds, for example, are used for community garden projects during the summer.

Ford Elementary School

1345 Mars Hill Road
Acworth, Georgia GA 30101
678-594-8092
www.cobbk12.org
Contact people: Jami Frost, principal; Catherine Padgett, teacher

If you are looking for a school that has a wide variety of outdoor enhancements, and is actively using them in highly creative ways, Ford Elementary is a must-see. The school has had an outdoor learning program since 1995. Just a few of the site elements include a nature trail, large hillside amphitheater, smaller outdoor classroom seating areas, children's garden, arboretum, individual raised classroom planting beds, native plant garden, aquatic features, bird feeding station, and themed gardens that nearly surround the building.

Ford is also an excellent example of a school with a well-planned volunteer program. The school's extensive Earth Parent program is described in Chapter 1.

The annual spring Evening in the Garden celebration is an amazing schoolwide event that fosters staff and community interest in outdoor learning. Student artwork and writing are showcased in the many outdoor classroom venues, and student musicians perform in the gardens. The playground is turned into an outdoor stage for an extravaganza with a cast of hundreds. Parents watch from the hillside overlooking the playground and enjoy food that they have brought with them or purchased at the site. Although many schools have a spring musical/arts event, the idea of centering the event in the outdoor classroom space is brilliant. Everyone gets the idea that learning and the outdoors mix beautifully.

It's worth a visit to Acworth just to meet Catherine Padgett, a driving force for outdoor learning in this building for fifteen years. Although she quickly and adamantly states that it takes many people to make Ford's outdoor education the success that it is, Catherine's dedication to outdoor learning has been pivotal. Not only is Catherine an outdoor learning advocate, she is skilled in public relations, grant writing, and community involvement.

Forest View Elementary

3007 Mt. Sinai Road
Durham, NC 27705
919-560-3932
www.dpsnc.net
Contact person: Neil Clay, principal

When you go to this school's Web site (http://www.forestview.dpsnc.net/), the home page has an intriguing link titled "Check out the outdoor learning initiative at Forest View." When you click on the link, you are taken to an excellent outdoor learning section that makes extensive use of pictures to illustrate outdoor learning experiences at Forest View. Links take you to more detailed information about various outdoor projects and venues that are provided at the school. Not only is Forest View doing great things with kids in the outdoors, the school is making it easy for parents and community members to see that schoolyard-enhanced learning is a part of the Forest View experience. It is refreshing to see outdoor learning highlighted right on the school's home page.

Forest View calls its outdoor teaching venues Outdoor Learning Spaces (OLS). Some of these outdoor learning spaces include a bird blind, labyrinth, nature trail, and wetland. A variety of gardens are found on the grounds, including a butterfly garden, classroom gardens, and an extensive kindergarten garden with specially designed raised beds.

At the front entrance to the school is the Using the Outdoors to Teach Experiential Science (UTOTES) garden. This garden was developed in collaboration with the North Carolina Museum of Natural Sciences and is frequently used by third graders. I really like the fact that an active garden/learning lab welcomes visitors as they approach the building. There also is a North Carolina Fourth Grade garden that includes indigenous plants that represent the many diverse areas of the state, from the mountains to the sea.

Forest View is a good example of a school that uses a wide variety of outdoor learning features throughout a range of grade levels. The school also has strategically placed many of its features so that visitors quickly get the sense that outdoor learning is important here.

The school has done an exemplary job of promoting and informing its constituents about outdoor learning through the addition of photos on the school Web site. The introduction at the top of the outdoor learning section of the Web site says it all: "This site is a guide to the outdoor learning centers that Forest View's faculty and students use on a regular basis to integrate all areas of the learning curriculum" (Forest View Elementary School 2010).

Granny's Garden School

20 Miamiview Drive
Loveland, OH 45140
513-324-2873
www.grannysgardenschool.com/index.html
Contact person: Roberta Paolo

Details about this highly innovative program and its founder, Roberta Paolo, are found in Spotlight 5, "Granny's Garden School." Granny's Garden School is not a public school building, but rather a nonprofit corporation that works with the public schools in Loveland, Ohio.

I include Granny's Garden School in this section because it is a unique and amazingly successful attempt to channel substantial outdoor learning assistance in the form of curriculum material, resource teachers, and materials to public schools through a nonprofit organization focused primarily on one school district. Since the help is coming from an external entity with a governing board and its own fund-raising initiatives, the potential certainly exists to keep the schoolyard enhancement efforts going long into the future. That the program is not tied to district funding facilitates flexibility and longevity.

By all means take a look at the extensive Web site of Granny's Garden School. Be sure to click on the "Programs" tab to get a flavor of the tremendous range of opportunities that this initiative provides. The types of school site enhancements and programming described there would be impossible for any school to provide and maintain without the help of an external organization like Granny's Garden School. Take a look, though, and see if there are perhaps a few elements that you could incorporate.

Finding Good Examples in Your Area

There are wonderful examples of schoolyard-enhanced learning taking place in every state and province. In Canada, the nonprofit organization Evergreen can provide information about exemplary programs occurring throughout the country. In the United States, there are several organizations that are in the process of collaborating to form a similar national information resource base about schoolyard learning success stories. In the interim, good information about exemplary outdoor learning is available from state departments of natural resources. Although organizational structures vary greatly by state, nearly all natural resource departments have a person or division that focuses on education. If you are looking for school sites to visit, start by exploring your state's department of natural resources Web site.

Another efficient way to find out about innovative outdoor learning in your area is to contact your state or provincial environmental education organization. The easiest way to find those state organizations is to go to the Web site of the North American Association for Environmental Education (NAAEE) at www.naaee.org. On the home page is a convenient link to "State and Provincial Affiliates." An interactive map of North America then provides contact information and a link to your local organization's Web site. Most state environmental organizations will be eager to provide names of schools in your area that are using the outdoors in creative ways.

Postscript

Writing this book provided a delightful opportunity to move beyond my comfort zone. You see, most of my previous work about outdoor learning has been based on my own prior experience as well as marvelous examples provided over the years by friends and associates. As the concept for *Moving the Classroom Outdoors* evolved, it was clear that visits to numerous schools and locations would be essential to provide a rich tapestry of examples showing schoolyard-enhanced learning in many venues. So began the schoolyard odyssey!

As I visited schools, I saw dozens of innovative and useful site enhancements and meaningful learning activities that utilized outdoor space in amazingly creative ways. Although the seating areas, gardens, and activity packets were impressive, I was most touched by the people I met. There were classroom teachers, administrators, support staff, and parent volunteers—already stretched by the routine demands of their jobs—willingly giving significant time and effort to promote outdoor learning. They didn't think in terms of hours or overtime; they evaluated their effort in terms of its tremendous impact upon students.

I have a vivid memory of touring a wonderful elementary school courtyard enhancement in Buffalo, New York. As a group of us toured this rich learning

space, the school's custodian was quietly standing off to the side, proudly smiling. Although we remarked to him that the site improvements probably translated into more work, he gently reminded us that this new space was "good for the children."

Seating and plantings, activities and curriculum connections all help to create meaningful outdoor learning experiences, but nothing of substance occurs unless inspired and inspiring people get involved. What makes things happen is enthusiastic "dreamstorming"—creatively thinking about possibilities and opportunities. It is my sincere hope that these pages will nourish your dreamstorming.

I would like to close this book with the same invitation that appeared in the postscript to *Schoolyard-Enhanced Learning*. If you are to be an advocate for the outdoors, you need to experience its beauty, complexity, and ability to soothe, revitalize, and even heal. It's my prayer that you will put this book down, go outside, and enthusiastically immerse yourself in the beauty of creation.

Treat yourself to a change of pace and place!

References

Allen, G. 1968. *Planning for Play*. London: Thames and Hudson.

Baker, Jeannie. 1991. *Window*. New York: Greenwillow Books.

Broda, Herbert W. 2007. *Schoolyard-Enhanced Learning: Using the Outdoors as an Instructional Tool, K–8*. Portland, ME: Stenhouse.

Brookside Elementary School. 2008. "The Schoolyard Enhanced Learning Program: An Elementary Renewal Proposal Submitted by Brookside Elementary School." Unpublished grant proposal. Worthington, OH: Brookside Elementary School.

Burns, Rebecca, and Donna Stoicovy. 2007. "Turning Learning Inside Out: A Contextualized Professional Development Plan." Unpublished paper.

Carson, Rachel. 1956. *The Sense of Wonder*. New York: Harper and Row.

Children and Nature Network. 2010. "About Us." http://www.childrenand nature.org/about/contact/.

Moving the Classroom Outdoors

Children and Nature Network. 2011. "Research and Publications." http://www.childrenandnature.org/research/.

Cofino, Kim. 2007. "Sign Me Up! The Elementary Email Solution: Linked Gmail Accounts." Always Learning. http://kimcofino.com/blog/2007/10/18/sign-me-up-the-elementary-email-solution-linked-gmail-accounts/.

D.C. Environmental Education Consortium. "Our Mission." D.C. Schoolyard Greening. http://www.dcschoolyardgreening.org.

Ehlert, Lois. 1988. *Planting a Rainbow*. San Diego, CA: Harcourt Brace Jovanovich.

———. 2005. *Leaf Man*. Orlando, FL: Harcourt.

Environmental Concern. 2010. "Who Is Environmental Concern? We're All About Wetlands." http://www.wetland.org/whoweare.htm.

Evergreen. 2010. "Who We Are." http://www.evergreen.ca/en/about/who-we-are.sn.

FCC (Federal Communications Commission). 2011. "Children's Internet Protection Act." http://www.fcc.gov/cgb/consumerfacts/cipa.html.

Forest View Elementary School. 2010. "Welcome to Forest View's Guide to Our Outdoor Learning Spaces." http://www.forestview.dpsnc.net/~outdoor_learning/Site/Welcome.html.

Frey FROGS 2005. *Adopt-a-Spot Handbook and Field Guide*. Acworth, GA: Frey Elementary PTSA. Available online at http://eealliance.org/assets/Documents/Initiatives/freyfrogsadopt-a-spothandbookpdfversion.pdf.

Fruit Tree Planting Foundation. 2005a. "Planting Fruit Trees for a Healthier Planet." http://www.ftpf.org.

Fruit Tree Planting Foundation. 2005b. "Fruit Tree 101." http://www.ftpf.org/fruittree101.htm.

FTC (Federal Trade Commission). 2011. "How to Comply with Children's On-line Privacy Protection Act." COPPA—Children's Online Privacy Protection Act. http://www.coppa.org/comply.htm.

Geocaching. 2011. "Welcome to Geocaching." http://www.geocaching.com.

Georgia Wildlife Federation. 2004. *Planning First to Make Your Outdoor Classroom Last: A Best Management Practices (BMP) Guide for Creating and Sustaining Outdoor Classrooms in Georgia.* Covington, GA: Georgia Wildlife Federation. Available online at http://97.67.50.31/resources/wildlifehabitats/bmps.pdf.

Global Gardens. 2010. "Welcome." http://www.global-gardens.org/index.php.

Google. 2011. "Google Search Basics: Basic Search Help." Google. http://www.google.com/support/websearch/bin/answer.py?hl=en&answer=134479.

Granny's Garden School. 2010a. "Mission." http://www.grannysgardenschool.com/100-1-00-mission.html.

Granny's Garden School. 2010b. "Teaching in the Garden Camp for School Garden Developers." Granny's Garden School. http://www.grannysgardenschool.com/152-0-00-educator-training-camp.html.

Leopold, Aldo. 1986. *A Sand County Almanac (Outdoor Essays and Reflections).* New York: Ballantine.

Lieberman, Gerald A., and Linda L. Hoody. 1998. *Closing the Achievement Gap: Using the Environment as an Integrating Context for Learning.* San Diego, CA: State Education and Environment Roundtable.

Louv, Richard. 2005. *Last Child in the Woods: Saving Our Children from Nature-Deficit Disorder.* Chapel Hill, NC: Algonquin.

Moving the Classroom Outdoors

Maryland Schoolyard Habitat Partnership. 2010. *Common Qualities of Excellent Schoolyard Habitats*. Available online at http://www.fws.gov/chesapeakebay/pdf/CommonQual4pp.pdf.

Meyer, Kirk. 2010. "Green Schoolyard Network: A Concept Paper." Green Schoolyard Network. http://greenschoolyardnetwork.org/2010/05/12/green-schoolyard-network-a-concept-paper/.

Most, Bernard. 1978. *If the Dinosaurs Came Back.* New York: Harcourt Brace Jovanovich.

National Wildlife Federation. 2011. "Certify Your Schoolyard Habitat." http://www.nwf.org/Get-Outside/Outdoor-Activities/Garden-for-Wildlife/Schoolyard-Habitats/Certify-Your-Schoolyard.aspx.

Orzolek, Michael. 1995. "Raised Garden Beds Offer Many Advantages." Press release. University Park: Pennsylvania State University Agricultural Information Service.

Payne, Ruby. 2005. *A Framework for Understanding Poverty*. Highlands, TX: aha! Process.

Place-Based Education Evaluation Collaborative. 2011. "Place-Based Ed. Research." http://www.peecworks.org/PEEC/PEEC_Research/.

Schiff, Paul. 1996. *Twenty/Twenty: Projects and Activities for Wild School Sites.* Columbus: Ohio Department of Natural Resources, Division of Wildlife.

Schulman, Alexis, and Catherine A. Peters. 2008. "GIS Analysis of Urban Schoolyard Landcover in Three U.S. Cities." *Urban Ecosystems* 11:65–80.

SFGSA (San Francisco Green Schoolyard Alliance). "Our Mission." http://sfgreenschools.org/.

University of Wisconsin Arboretum. 2009. *Earth Partnership for Schools: Facilitator Handbook.* Madison: University of Wisconsin Arboretum.

USFWS (U.S. Fish and Wildlife Service). 2010. *Schoolyard Habitat Project Guide.* Available online at http://www.fws.gov/ChesapeakeBay/pdf/habitatguide.pdf. (Revised version is available at http://www.fws.gov/cno/conservation/schoolyard.cfm.)

Wisconsin Fast Plants. 2010. "Introduction to Fast Plants." Wisconsin Fast Plants Program, University of Wisconsin–Madison. http://www.fastplants.org/intro.php.

Wood, Karan. 2006. "The Field of Dreams (and other Outdoor Classroom Myths)." *Green Teacher* 79:35–39.

Wurdinger, Scott. 1997. *Philosophical Issues in Adventure Education.* Dubuque, IA: Kendall/Hunt.

Wyzga, Marilyn. 2001. "Funding Schoolyard Projects." In *Greening School Grounds: Creating Habitats for Learning*, edited by Tim Grant and Gail Littlejohn, 19–21. Toronto: Green Teacher.

Index